UNIVERSITY OF WINNIPEG

LIBRARY

THE
MOIRA BELL
COLLECTION

Presented by
Mr. and Mrs. Herbert M. Bell
in memory of their daughter

MOIRA ANN

1946 - 1969

THOMAS CAMPION

Poet, Composer, Physician

Other works by Edward Lowbury

✱

TIME FOR SALE
DAYLIGHT ASTRONOMY

THOMAS CAMPION

Poet, Composer, Physician

BY

EDWARD Joseph Lister LOWBURY

TIMOTHY SALTER

AND

ALISON YOUNG

1970

CHATTO & WINDUS

LONDON

Published by
Chatto & Windus Ltd
40 William IV Street
London W.C.2

*

Clarke, Irwin & Co. Ltd
Toronto

SBN 7011 1477 0

Printed in Great Britain by
R. & R. Clark Ltd
Edinburgh

CONTENTS

ILLUSTRATIONS

PREFACE

IN 1967 the quatercentenary of the birth of Thomas Campion passed almost unnoticed. This is surprising when we consider his reputation as one of the finest English lyrical poets and his unique position as one who set his own poetry to music of similar excellence. Students of song and of the relation of words to music have found the dual rôle of Campion instructive, and a number of studies have been written on this subject; the authors have usually approached their subject either from a literary or from a musical angle; but Campion's range of gifts and activities was so great that a balanced view of his work cannot be obtained except by a planned approach from several angles – literary, musical, even medical.

The authors of this study have attempted such a multilateral survey of Campion's work. Their aim has been to examine how the same mind expresses the same idea in music and in poetry, to explore the range of Campion's English poems and to consider the rôle of various influences, including Campion's theories of composition and his practice of medicine, on the nature of his creative work.

The quotations from Campion's works are given in the original spelling, as presented in Vivian's edition (1909), except for 'u' and 'v', which are used as in modern spelling. In the musical examples we have replaced the assortment of C and G clefs used by Campion in the notation of the vocal line by the G clef. Original note-values and barring have been retained, except for the barring of *Vaine men whose follies* (see p. 167ᵉ). The original key-signatures have also been retained (in one instance with the order of flats 'corrected'), although it should be remembered that often they do not indicate the tonality of the music as key-signatures do today. Cautionary accidentals in brackets are editorial. The original time-signatures are included only where the complete songs have been quoted. They do not have the same function as a modern time-signature, but indicate primarily whether the metre is duple or triple. The underlay of the words has been clarified by the addition of slurs where two or more notes are sung to one syllable. For our sources of the airs we have used the original editions at the British Museum (K.2.i.3, K.2.i.1, K.2.i.2) and also Fellowes' edition (Stainer & Bell).

We are deeply grateful to Mr. Robert Gittings and to Mr. David Greer for many valuable comments on the text of this book; to Dr. Nigel Fortune for helpful suggestions; to the Librarians of the British Museum, the Bodleian, Gray's Inn, and the Royal College of Physicians for their help and for permission to reproduce certain prints and manuscripts; and to the Director of the National Portrait Gallery for permission to reproduce the painting shown facing page 25 (Plate 2).

ABBREVIATIONS USED IN THE TEXT

RBI Philip Rosseter's *A Booke of Ayres*: first part, by Thomas Campion

RBII Philip Rosseter's *A Booke of Ayres*: second part, by Philip Rosseter

I *Two Bookes of Ayres*, by Thomas Campion: the first book (*Divine and Morall Songs*)

II *Two Bookes of Ayres*, by Thomas Campion: the second book (*Light Conceits of Lovers*)

III *The Third Booke of Ayres*, by Thomas Campion

IV *The Fourth Booke of Ayres*, by Thomas Campion

PMLA Publications of the Modern Language Association of America

I

POSTHUMOUS FORTUNES

A CHARACTERISTIC feature of Elizabethan life was the cult of versatility. The balanced man was admired, the one whose wit, in the words of Roger Ascham, 'is quicke without lightnes, sharpe without brittlenes, desirous of good thinges without newfangle-nes, diligent in painfull thinges without werisomnes, and constant in good will to do all thinges well'.[1] This ideal was connected with a world picture of Order which the Renaissance inherited from the Middle Ages;[2] it was felt that Man should, in a sense, be a microcosm of the Universe around him. A proper balance of the basic qualities or 'mixing of the Elements' in Man was thought to be attainable by a curriculum in which learning was mixed with singing, playing on instruments, and a variety of 'comely exercises'.

This training certainly encouraged versatility, and emphasised the importance of music and poetry; an ability to sing at sight was accepted as a normal social accomplishment, and the ability and desire to versify was probably as common. Outstanding gifts in several different fields, however, were rare then as they are today. In Campion's words (which contain an echo of Ascham) 'All doe not all things well';[3] but it was Campion who more nearly than most of his contemporaries did achieve this ideal. His name, it is true, rings small beside those of a number of celebrated Elizabethans, and in versatility he is approached, if not matched, by Sidney, Raleigh and Francis Bacon. His art is that of a miniaturist, to be compared with the work of his con-temporary Nicholas Hilliard, not with the epics of Leonardo and Michelangelo; but the varied forms in which these giants—and

[1] *The Scholemaster*, 1570 (English Reprints, No. 23, Edward Arber, London, 1870, p. 37).
[2] See E. M. W. Tillyard, *The Elizabethan World Picture*, Chatto & Windus, London, 1952.
[3] This resembles Virgil's phrase 'Non omnia possumus omnes' (*Eclogues*, VIII, 64) quoted by Campion in the preface of *Two Bookes of Ayres* (*Campion's Works*, edited by P. Vivian, Oxford, 1909, p. 114).

1

Goethe three hundred years later–expressed themselves were essentially separate channels of their creative imagination. Campion's music and poetry, by contrast, flowed in a single stream. His creative gifts were almost perfectly integrated, and illustrate well the Renaissance ideals of balance and order.

The works on which Campion's reputation today is most securely founded are the airs for solo voice with accompaniment for lute or lute with viola da gamba. These airs are exceptional in that the words and the music are known to have been written for each other by the same hand; what is rarer, both are highly praised, some claiming that the words cannot be fully appreciated or even scanned without the music, others regarding the poetry as what matters most and outstanding of its kind. Poets have praised the words and musicians have praised the music. If he had left nothing but these airs Campion would still be exceptional in his mastery of two distinct art forms, but his talents carried him far into other fields. His *Observations in the Art of English Poesie* is one of the classics of criticism, and one which stimulated much heated discussion. More influential, if less controversial, was the treatise *A New Way of making fowre Parts in Counter-point*, which was reprinted long after his death as a section in several editions of Playford's *Introduction to the Skill of Musick*, for many years a standard reference work on musical theory. An appreciable part of Campion's literary output consisted of Latin poems in which he shows a mastery of form and intimacy with Roman poetry–Catullus, Propertius and Martial in particular. The four Masques are ranked with those of Ben Jonson, and in these again Campion used both his musical and his poetic talents to achieve a fine synthesis. While engaged in these artistic and literary pursuits he practised medicine in London and appears to have won a good reputation as a doctor.

The evidence suggests that he was well known in his lifetime. In 1593, when Campion was twenty-six years old, George Peele paid a tribute to his poems, which were still unpublished, by making the following reference to him in the prologue of *The Honour of the Garter*:[1]

---

[1] *The Works of Peele* (ed. Bullen), Vol. II, John Nimmo, London, 1888, p. 319.

Augustus long ago hath left the world,
And liberal Sidney, famous for the love
He bare to learning and to chivalry,
And virtuous Walsingham are fled to heaven . . .
Why thither speeds not Rosamond's trumpeter,
Sweet as the nightingale? Why goest not thou
That richly cloth'st conceit in well-made words,
Campion . . .

By 'Rosamond's trumpeter' he means Samuel Daniel. Daniel,[1] in his reply to Campion's *Observations*, opens the attack with a compliment: 'this detractor (whose commendable rhymes, albeit now himself an enemy to Rhyme, have given heretofore to the world the best notice of his worth) is a man of fair parts and good reputation.' To Campion, who called his English poems 'eare-pleasing rimes without Arte', the implicit slight upon his 'deeper studies' may have outweighed the compliment; but there were some who found the highest praise for Campion's Latin poems, notably Charles FitzGeffrey, who wrote a eulogy of Campion in Latin elegiacs, and Francis Meres who made a favourable comparison of the Latin verse of Campion (and of some other Englishmen) with classical Latin poetry. As a composer Campion achieved some of his greatest public success in being commissioned four times to write masques for the nobility. Recognition of Campion's versatility is shown in a sonnet from John Davies of Hereford's *Scourge of Folly*:

TO THE MOST JUDITIOUS AND EXCELLENT
LYRICK-POET, DOCTOR CAMPION

Upon my selfe I should just vengeance take
Should I omitt thy mention in my Rimes,
Whose Lines and Notes do lullaby (awake)
In Heavens of pleasure, these unpleasant Times.

Never did Lyrick's more than happie straines,
(Straind out of Arte by nature, so with ease),
So purely hitt the moods and various Vaines
Of musick and her Hearers as do These.

[1] 'A Defence of Ryme', 1603 (in *English Critical Essays* (ed. E. D. Jones), Oxford, 1943, p. 73).

So thou canst cure the Body and the minde,
(Rare Doctor,) with thy twofold soundest Arte;
Hippocrates hath taught thee the one kinde,
Apollo and the Muse the other Part;

And both so well that thou with both dost please,
The Minde, with pleasure, and the *Corps*, with ease.

But the crowning tribute came from the great historian,
William Camden, in a passage written in 1605, when most of
Campion's works had not yet been published; speaking of poets
old and new, he says, 'If I would come to our own time, what
a world could I present to you out of Sir Philipp Sidney,
Ed. Spencer, Samuel Daniel, Hugh Holland, Ben. Jonson,
Th. Campion, Mich. Drayton, George Chapman, John Marston,
William Shakespeare and other most pregnant witts of these
times, whom succeeding ages may justly admire.'[1]

Succeeding ages, however, lost sight of Campion's music and
poetry. One song, the unforgettable *Never weather-beaten Saile*,
is thought to have survived as a hymn at least until 1707, in
which year it is found transcribed in a commonplace book;
another song (*What if a day*) appears from reference to it in
Butler's *Hudibras* to have been popular still in 1663. So far as we
can tell, little or nothing was heard of the others until the later
years of the nineteenth century. Vivian attributes the eclipse of
the song books of Campion and others to the Puritan ascendancy
'with its hatred of music, especially secular music'.[2] But while
the Puritans may have put some musicians out of work, they
were far more tolerant of music than of the drama. Milton loved
music–'soft Lydian airs' no less than 'service high and anthems
clear', and Cromwell was something of a connoisseur. Henry
Lawes, the song writer whom Milton praised for his setting of
English verse, flourished during the Commonwealth, and in the
evolution of his work from the lute song tradition to the baroque
idiom he reflected changes which were quite unrelated to Puri-
tanism. These changes, which carried away the full glory of
Elizabethan and Jacobean music, were part of a European movement away from polyphony and from the ecclesiastical influences

[1] *Remaines of a Greater Worke Concerning Britaine, 1605* (quoted in
Campion's Works (ed. Vivian), Oxford, 1909, p. xxxviii).
[2] *Campion's Works* (ed. Vivian), Oxford, 1909, p. lviii.

which had dominated music since the Middle Ages. The characteristic expression of the movement was the birth of opera in Italy and its rapid spread to other countries; England was not the last to follow this lead, and the Puritans raised no objection to the unfrivolous new art. During those years, too, music and letters took on a more professional and specialised character, and the old tradition that a lyric is a poem to be sung fell into abeyance. From now on the two arts went their own ways. We can see this trend already in Ben Jonson's attitude on the reading of poetry; speaking of King James he says 'Buchanan [his tutor] had corrupted his ears when young, and learned him to sing verses when he should have read them'.[1]

One might suppose the lute song, which is the least polyphonic music of the Elizabethan period, would stand a better chance of weathering these changes of taste than the other musical forms; its eclipse as an independent form,[2] however, was more complete and prolonged than that of the madrigal, which achieved a mild revival in the eighteenth century. The Elizabethans treated song lyrics as things of little account, and did not usually publish the name of the poet on the printed score of a song. From their appearance in poetry books and miscellanies, some of the song poems are recognised as the work of Sidney, Spenser, Shakespeare, Fulke Greville and others, but most of them have remained anonymous to this day. Campion's work is the outstanding exception; but although his name is attached to the words as well as the music, the eclipse of Campion's airs was as complete as that of the other lutenist song books. Being printed in music books the poetry remained in hiding during the late eighteenth and early nineteenth centuries when such works as *England's Helicon* and *A Paradyse of Daintye Devises* again saw the light and Elizabethans enjoyed a new respectability.

Some idea of the process which swept away the music of Campion and his contemporaries can be gathered from Roger North's *The Musicall Gramarian*, written in 1728. In a survey which reveals much ignorance of the period of Byrd and Gibbons, North blamed

the magistratical censures of the present times, most fluently

---

[1] Marchette Chute, *Ben Jonson of Westminster*, London, 1954, p. 119.
[2] Though the lute song died out, the air has a continuous history (Lawes, Purcell, etc.).

cast upon all that men formerly did, as if they had bin ideots
and no art belonged to them. This so generall abrenonciation
of all elder tho' lately bygone musick, [he continues], is the
caus that almost all the ancient copys, tho very finely wrote,
are lost and gone, and that little which is left by pastry and
wast paper uses is wearing out, and in a short time none at
all will be left.[1]

North was the child of his time when he criticised the examples
of Tudor part-writing, in particular the *in nomines*, that came his
way 'because there is no scheme or design in it, for beginning,
middle and ending are all alike'; but he found more virtue in the
'lighter ayres for songs and dances, such as they (like us) thought
(as we think ours) incomparable'.[2] He then speaks of the rise of
Alfonso Ferrabosco, Coperario 'and others as may be found in
the old Musick books and were deservedly famous'.

   Roger North's fear that all copies of the earlier music would
soon be destroyed was, fortunately, ill-founded. Sir John Hawkins's *History of the Science and Practice of Music*, published in
1776, showed that a large body of Elizabethan and Jacobean
music was accessible to those who looked for it, and his book
contains a surprising amount of information on the lives and
music of Tallis, Byrd, Morley, Wilbye, Weelkes, Bull, Orlando
Gibbons and many others, including Thomas Campion. Hawkins
is sparing in expression of opinion; there is, for example, some
rather mild praise of the madrigals, but the music of Dowland
and Campion is mentioned without comment. There is a footnote
giving some details of Campion's work as poet, musician, theorist
and writer of masques. Dr. Charles Burney, whose *General History of Music* also appeared first in 1776 and had more influence
in its day than Hawkins's *History*, is more outspoken. Burney
could see some merit in the Elizabethan madrigals, but considered
the airs 'more dry, fanciless and frivolous'. His attitude is well
illustrated in the following remarks about Dowland:

> After being at the pains of scoring several of Dowland's
> compositions, I have been equally disappointed and aston-
> ished at his scanty abilities in counterpoint, and the great

[1] Roger North, *The Musicall Gramarian* (ed. H. Andrews), Oxford
University Press, 1925, p. 4.
[2] Roger North, op. cit., p. 10.

reputation he acquired with his contemporaries, which has been courteously continued to him, either by indolence or ignorance of those who have had occasion to speak of him, and who took it for granted that his title to fame, as a profound musician, was well founded.[1]

Burney refers also to the airs of William Corkine, Robert Jones and John Daniel, 'all obscure musicians and of mean abilities'; and of Ferrabosco (the son) he says that his airs 'have little merit of any kind', and yet were dedicated 'with no great humility' to Prince Henry. It is in connection with Ferrabosco's airs that we find a reference to Campion: 'three herald minstrels, ycleped Ben Jonson, T. Campion and N. Tomkins, proclaimed the high worth and qualities of these ayres in three encomiastic copies of verses prefixed to the work; but these friendly bards,who praised not with a very sparing hand, seem to have less exalted ideas of the author's merit and importance, than himself.'[2] There is no mention of Campion's music.

A modern reader of such views may marvel at their blindness or perversity, but the position seemed very different in the seventeenth and eighteenth centuries when new worlds of instrumental and dramatic expression were suddenly revealed to lovers of music. These developments culminated in the great personal utterances of Bach, Handel, Haydn and Mozart. In England, after the period when Blow and Purcell were contributing a valuable share to this ferment, musical imagination suffered a decline. Those who were interested in music drew their ideals from abroad. With one of the greatest of foreign musicians in their midst—indeed, naturalised—English musicians may not have sensed any departure from the main stream of European musical development; on the contrary, they must have felt that in imitating Handel they were in the movement. The decay of taste which came in the following century may have had its roots in this renunciation of the native tradition, but that is a separate story. In the meantime there poured into England a profusion of large-scale works—operas from Italy, sonatas and symphonies from Germany and Austria—and musical life was rich. It is no

[1] *A General History of Music*, by Charles Burney (ed. F. Mercer), G. T. Foulis, London, 1935, Vol. 2, p. 117.
[2] Op cit., p. 118.

wonder, then, that Dr. Burney and his contemporaries were content to live in the present, and treated with impatience English songs of an earlier time, 'which' (to quote Dr. Burney again) 'had only a single accompaniment for lute or viol'.

At about the same time as the change of taste in music, a neo-classic movement in the world of letters was gathering power, especially in France and in England, and taste in literature changed as radically as it did in music. Eyes were suddenly opened—or so it seemed—to the shortcomings and crudities of earlier writers—the Elizabethan poets, for example. Dryden regarded this as a question of growing up: 'We must be children before we grow Men. There was an Ennius, and in process of time a Lucilius, and a Lucretius, before Virgil and Horace; even after Chaucer there was a Spenser, a Harington, a Fairfax, before Waller and Denham were in being; and our Numbers were in their nonage till these last appeared.'[1] Atterbury was even more direct: 'Verse before Waller was downright prose tagged with rhyme.'[2] Even Shakespeare came in for severe treatment by Rymer, who found 'the neighing of a horse or the howling of a mastiff possesses more meaning' than the verse of Othello[3]; but Shakespeare, and Elizabethan dramatists generally, had more sympathetic treatment than the non-dramatic poets, whose work was, for the most part, ignored. A list of 'the best English poets' in Edward Bysshe's *Art of English Poetry* (1700) includes 47 names, but there is no mention of any non-dramatic poet before Cowley. Eighty years later Johnson begins his *Lives of the most celebrated English Poets* with Cowley. Pope, like his master Dryden, had something like veneration for Shakespeare but he despised

> The mob of gentlemen who wrote with ease;
> Sprat, Carew, Sedley and a hundred more,
> (Like twinkling stars the Miscellanies o'er).[4]

It is hardly surprising that the Elizabethan and Jacobean lyric was ignored during the late seventeenth and eighteenth centuries. Criticism at that time was largely preoccupied with the epic and

---

[1] 'Preface to the Fables', 1700 (in *English Critical Essays*, ed. E. D. Jones, 1943, p. 220).

[2] See G. Saintsbury, *A History of Criticism*, 1928, Vol. 2, p. 449.

[3] G. Saintsbury, op. cit., p. 397.

[4] *Imitations of Horace*, Epistle 1, 107–109.

the drama, and even contemporary lyrical poetry received little attention. In fact, Hobbes refused the title of poem to 'sonets, epigrams, eclogues and like pieces which are but essayes and parts of an entire Poem'.[1] For some account of the song books and miscellanies we must turn, significantly, to the historian of music, and again we find Hawkins quite well-informed and slightly less non-committal than he is when speaking of the music. The words of the songs, he tells us, were 'by writers little known to the world, the authors of madrigals, sonnets and other compositions for music, many whereof will be found to have great merit'.[2] He refers to *A Paradyse of Daintye Devises* and *England's Helicon*, and gives a list of the poets whose works were printed in the latter. Dr. Burney's attitude to the poetry of the madrigals is in keeping with his opinion of some of the music: 'We should suppose from the words of these madrigals that our Lyric Poetry, which has never been much cultivated by real judges and lovers of music, was in a state of utter barbarism when they were written, if the sonnets of Spenser and Shakespeare did not bear testimony to the contrary.'[3]

The Romantic Movement brought with it a fresh interest in Shakespeare and some reawakening to the merits of Elizabethan poetry. As early as 1765 Percy had included a number of Elizabethan and Jacobean lyrics in his *Reliques of Ancient English Poetry*, and Brydges made available a wider selection, including *England's Helicon*, in *The British Bibliographer* (*1810*). Hazlitt could see in the lyrical poetry of Drayton, Drummond and others some of the 'uncouthness' which made it repellent to Augustan critics, but found that 'it as often wore a sylph-like form with Attic vest, with faery feet, and the butterfly's gaudy wings'.[4] In their devotion to Nature, the Romantic critics were ill at ease either with the rhetoric of Sidney or with the metaphysical brainwork of Donne. Far-fetched images were unnatural, and poetry was not to be mixed with prose. Coleridge expresses the dilemma by stating that he had found in the Jacobean poets 'the most

[1] Preface to William Davenant's *Gondibert*; in *Critical Essays of the Seventeenth Century* (ed. Spingarn), Oxford, 1908.
[2] *A General History of the Science and Practice of Music*, Vol. 3, p. 417, by Sir John Hawkins, London, 1776.
[3] C. Burney, op. cit., Vol. 2, p. 113.
[4] W. Hazlitt, *Lectures on the Literature of the Age of Elizabeth*, London, George Bell, 1899, p. 174.

B

fantastic thoughts, in the most correct and natural language', while
more recent versifiers were too often characterised by the opposite
fault of conveying 'in the most fantastic language the most trivial
thoughts'.[1]

Campion's poems were safely hidden with their music during
those unmusical days. Had they been read, they might have
attracted interest; but it seems at least as probable that they
would have been considered too calculated and artificial, and
perhaps too frivolous, by such critics as Wordsworth or Coleridge or Shelley. It is no great step from Campion to Herrick,
and speaking of that 'new discovery' Hazlitt found that he had
'little of the spirit of love and wine; and from his frequent
allusion to pearls and rubies one might take him for a lapidary
instead of a poet . . . now this is making a petrifaction of love
and poetry'.[2]

As poet and composer, then, Campion was forgotten soon
after his death, and his memory was left undisturbed during the
storm and stress of the Romantic Movement. His reputation as a
musical theorist, however, lived on through the seventeenth
century. The repeated publication of his *New Way of Making
Fowre Parts in Counter-point* was evidence of its continued useful-
ness, since the leaders of the new movement were not in the habit
of preserving specimens of the old style for sentimental reasons.
Campion had something to communicate to those who found
Byrd and Gibbons old-fashioned; in fact, the novelty of his thesis
lies in the emphasis which it lays on the vertical or harmonic
structure, a development which was much to the taste of musicians during the Commonwealth and after the Restoration. In
contrast, Morley's more celebrated *Plaine and Easie Introduction
to Practicall Musicke* (1597) presented an account of the subject
which may have seemed outmoded when Campion's ideas were
still in fashion, and the book was only reissued once (in 1608)
during the seventeenth century.

There were signs of a growing interest in the song books and
their poetry for some time before the 'rediscovery'. In 1837, for
example, Thomas Oliphant, the secretary of the Madrigal Society,
published his anthology, *La Musa Madrigalesca—Madrigals,
Ballads and Roundelays chiefly of the Elizabethan Age.* This

[1] S. T. Coleridge, *Biographia Literaria*, 1817, London, George Bell, 1882,
p. 193.   [2] W. Hazlitt, op. cit., p. 194.

included one poem by Campion (*There is a Garden in her face*), which was reprinted anonymously with other poems from Richard Alison's *An Howre's Recreation in Musicke*. There is also a large selection of lyrics from the songbooks of Dowland. The editor makes few comments on the words, but he agrees with Dr. Burney in finding Dowland's music unworthy of its reputation, 'for however beautiful most of his madrigals may be as to melody, they are little else than harmonised airs'; apparently it never occurred to Oliphant that Dowland might have preferred his airs not to seem like madrigals, even if performers were offered the traditional choice of singing them in parts. In 1838 William Chappell published his *Collection of National English Airs*, in which appeared the words and music of one song each by Dowland, Ford and Morley, and it contains an anonymous song with words by Campion (whose name is not mentioned). This collection formed the basis of Chappell's magnum opus, *Popular Music of the Olden Time* (1859), and this in turn was revised and renamed by H. E. Wooldridge in 1893.

By that time, however, the words of the madrigals and lute songs had been offered to a wider audience by other collectors. The first of these was Edward Arber, who reprinted in *An English Garner* the complete words of the airs by Campion and Dowland, and also those of the first three sets of madrigals by Byrd, of *The Triumphs of Oriana*, of Yonge's first *Musica Transalpina*, and of madrigal books by Wilbye and Alison. This anthology, which appeared in six volumes between 1879 and 1890, contains a wide range of verse and prose which, as its editor remarks, 'hardly anyone would imagine to be in existence at all'. The *Garner* was collected from rare books and manuscripts in the British Museum and elsewhere, and is presented as 'a study of detached areas of English history'. The authors— often strangely assorted—are allowed to speak for themselves without editorial comment. In 1886 A. H. Bullen first published his well-known *Lyrics from the Elizabethan Song Books*, which gave prominence to Campion, and in 1889 he issued the first collected edition of *The Works of Doctor Thomas Campion*, including the airs, the masques, *Observations in the Art of English Poesie*, the Latin epigrams and elegies and some other English verse.

Bullen's enthusiasm was contagious, and the poems of the

song books–especially those of Campion–were soon taken up with intensity and sometimes (as Bullen later hinted) with un-critical adulation. In George Saintsbury's *History of English Literature* (1887) the poetry of the song books is called 'a body of verse as probably could not be got together . . . in any other quarter-century of any nation's history'. The poets are treated collectively, and there is no reference to Campion in the index, but of the nine examples of verse from the song books quoted, four are by Campion. Ernest Rhys, in 1895, describes Campion as 'perhaps the one poet who comes nearest to fulfilling, in the genre and quality of his work, the lyric canon in English poetry'.[1] The enthusiasm had not faded by 1912, when Andrew Lang spoke of Campion as 'one of the most delightful singers in the whole of English literature';[2] or in 1932, when T. S. Eliot described him as 'except for Shakespeare, the most accomplished master of rhymed lyric of his time'.[3] Nor did the changes of literary fashion during the thirties and forties shake Campion's re-established stature as a poet. In 1954, for example, C. S. Lewis writes 'with one exception his poems can be divided only into the good and the better, or else into the more and less characteristic'.[4]

Although the song books were rediscovered at the time of England's musical renascence, and possibly under the influence of that movement, it was their poetry that was first appreciated. The collections of Campion's works edited by Bullen (1889), Rhys (1895) and Vivian (1909) were devoted to the verse and prose writings, and the poems were commended primarily for their literary excellence; indeed Bullen was reported by Yeats to have hated music. It was not until 1920, when Edmund Fellowes began his pioneer work of publishing the song books with their music, that the lutenist composers were rescued from the ob-scurity of rare and sometimes unique copies. The excellence of the lute songs was immediately recognised. Fellowes places their composers in the highest rank of song writers, and regards Campion as being 'with the exception of Dowland the most

[1] *The Lyric Poems of Thomas Campion* (ed. Ernest Rhys), Dent, 1895.
[2] *History of English Literature*, London, 1912, p. 290.
[3] *The Use of Poetry and the Use of Criticism*, Faber & Faber, London, 1932, p. 37.
[4] *English Literature of the Sixteenth Century*, Oxford, 1954, p. 552.

important of the lutenist song writers'.[1] W. H. Hadow also ranked Campion near to Dowland.[2] Others–for example, Peter Warlock[3]–have suggested that Campion, for all his charm as a tune-maker, did not approach Dowland in excellence and was too often content with complacently four-square songs of the conventional hymn-tune pattern. Warlock is taken to task for this view by Gustave Reese, who considers that Campion's excellence in the literary field has obscured his musical excellence; 'his songs have achieved less attention than they deserve, musicographers being too severe in charging them with superficiality'.[4]

The interest taken in Campion's other activities during his second period of fame is, to some extent, dependent on the vitality of his reputation as a poet and song writer. The Latin poems, which were his pride, are read (if ever) for the light they throw on his life and times, not for their poetic interest. His prose writings, however, have more life of their own. The *Observations* are reprinted as a classic and curiosity of literary criticism. The treatise on counterpoint is of considerable historic interest for reasons which we have mentioned; Warlock goes further and suggests that it might well be used today by students of composition in preference to many a modern textbook! The masques, apart from the airs contained in them, have not been restored to life, though they bring back with vividness the pomp of King James's court. Their significance for us, however,–at least as examples of a type–goes further than this; for while the lute songs, which seem so advanced to us in retrospect, were swept away on the tide of change, the masque was evolving into ballet and opera, and influencing the presentation of drama. Considered in this light, Campion's masques assume a new interest, for they give exceptional prominence to music and were scored for quite an impressive orchestra. The historical interest of such dated works is therefore hardly less than that of Campion's lasting contribution, which came at the end of a line of development in the art of song and had little influence on what was to follow.

---

[1] Preface to Campion's Airs in *Rosseter's Book of Airs*, Stainer & Bell, London, 1922. A new edition of this series is appearing, edited by Thurston Dart.   [2] *Music*, Butterworth, London, 1924.

[3] *The English Ayre*, O.U.P., London, 1926, p. 105.

[4] *Music in the Renaissance*, London, 1954, p. 839.

2

QUIET PILGRIMAGE

T H E available facts about Campion give us no more than glimpses of the man at different times of his life; but in this he was of his age which, for all its panegyrics on Fame, did not cultivate biography. We must reconstruct what we can from a jumble of disconnected details; from parish registers, legal documents, account books, Latin epigrams (often obscure), dedications and pamphlets.[1] In the case of Campion it adds up to rather more than we know about most of the other song writers and lyrical poets of that unique generation.

He was born in London on Ash Wednesday, 12th February 1567, three years after Shakespeare and four after John Dowland. His baptism on the next day is recorded in the parish register of St. Andrew's, Holborn–the parish where, two hundred years later, Thomas Chatterton was buried. We can see this church today near Holborn Circus (at least, the one which Wren built in 1684, incorporating part of the original building). Nearby are other relics of Campion's London: Staple Inn, which survived the Fire to remind us how London looked then, and Gray's Inn, where Campion studied, with its sixteenth-century hall (see plate 1). Near the junction of Cursitor Street and Chancery Lane stood a house 'built with divers fair lodgings for gentlemen, all of brick and timber'.[2] It was here that the 'cursitors' or clerks of the Court of Chancery worked and lived, one of them being John Campion, who can with some confidence be identified as the poet's father; and here, according to Vivian's conjecture, Thomas Campion lived till he was nine years old with his parents, his sister Rose and his stepsister, Mary Trigg.

John Campion's family came from the village of Anstey in

---

[1] Much of this knowledge we owe to the studies of Percival Vivian, which are described in the Introduction to his edition of *Campion's Works*, Oxford, 1909.

[2] *Campion's Works* (ed. Vivian), Oxford, 1909, p. xiv; and Stow's *Survey of London*, 1603 (ed. Wheatley), London, 1956, p. 390.

Hertfordshire, but his father (Thomas' grandfather) is said to have lived in Dublin. In 1564, according to Chester's *London Marriage Licences*, 'John Campion,[1] gent., of St. Clement Danes' obtained a marriage licence on 21st June and was married at St. Andrew's, Holborn, on 26th June to Lucy Trigg, a widow'. This is the first record we have of Thomas Campion's father. In 1565 he was admitted to the Middle Temple. From the next year he was employed with eighteen other cursitors in drawing up writs for the Chancery Court, earning a comfortable salary. By 1569 he was sufficiently well off to buy Aveley Parsonage, near Purfleet, while holding other property and renting farms in Wiltshire. He was elected vestryman at St. Andrew's in 1573. In the zeal for social betterment he sketched a coat of arms with what might be taken for a campion flower at its centre, but there is no record that this was accepted by the College of Heralds. He died in 1576, and was buried at St. Andrew's, Holborn.

His wife, Lucy Campion, cuts a more striking, if still indistinct, figure. The daughter of Laurence Searle, a Serjeant-at-Arms attending on the Sovereign, she brought worldly goods as well as an aura of gentility to her three marriages. The first husband, Roger Trigg, was an Attorney of the Common Pleas practising in London. They had one child, Mary. Roger Trigg died in 1563. Perhaps John Campion, another lawyer, had moved in their circle. When she married him in 1564, Lucy had inherited property from her grandfather and from Roger Trigg, and shortly afterwards she received a legacy from her father. This sudden wealth must have helped John Campion to better his position–he probably owed his appointment at the Middle Temple to it; but he also found himself burdened with much litigation on his wife's behalf.

When John Campion died, Lucy moved with her three children from London to her late husband's house at Brokenborough in Wiltshire; but in less than a year she was back in Holborn for a third marriage. The new husband, one Augustine Steward, was well-off and well-connected. Like Lucy's earlier husbands he was a lawyer, and apparently a former friend of the Campion household. Two days before the marriage (in 1577) Lucy signed

---

[1] The family name is spelt here with an 'o' as it is in the extant signature and in all the English publications of Thomas Campion except his four *Books of Ayres*, where he spells it 'Campian'.

a contract making over to Steward all her possessions, but stipulating that certain sums of money should go to her children: to Mary Trigg, fifty pounds; to Rose Campion, two hundred pounds at her marriage, and to Thomas Campion the choice of an annuity of forty pounds per annum or a single payment of two hundred and sixty pounds (he chose the latter). Rose was still unmarried and living with the Stewards in 1592. From Augustine's meticulous household accounts we learn that Lucy had lent much of her money to the poor relatives of John Campion and others; also that the children received a legacy from one Alice Bendbrig. This did not amount to much; Thomas, for example, was left 'a basin, an ewer, a quart wine pot and a damask napkin', and some vague interest in the residue of her estate. In 1580 Lucy died, and in the next year Augustine married again, his new wife, Anne Sisley, bringing him another stepson by her former marriage.

So in his fourteenth year Thomas Campion found himself with two foster-parents, something of an outsider in his own home. It is likely that such a restless background had an effect on his personality and later development – in encouraging self-reliance, for example, and in prompting an unsentimental view of life: he wrote amorous verse, but remained single. Not inconsistent with this attitude was his cultivation of classical virtues and precision (though the disciplinarian in him may have owed something positive to the legal background of his home). By two deeds which Thomas signed while he was at Gray's Inn (in 1587 and 1588), Augustine secured undisputed tenure of Lucy's property, and yet when he died, in 1595, he made no mention of Thomas in his will. He had fulfilled his legal obligations as a guardian, and Thomas was on good enough terms to witness several documents for him; but there is no hint of affection between them, and no recognisable mention of Augustine in the Epigrams where many friendships are recorded.

We are in the dark about Thomas' early education. Schools in Holborn which he may have attended were the Grammar School of St. Andrew's and the Mercers' School (known then as St. Thomas of Acon's). In the summer of 1581 he went up to Peterhouse, Cambridge, his half-brother Thomas Sisley following him in the autumn. He remained at the College until 1584 and left without taking a degree. From Steward's account book we learn that the sum spent each year to keep Campion and Sisley at Cambridge–including their University dues–was £20. The boys shared a bedroom, but each had his own study. From the fact that their expenses were calculated on the basis of fifty-two weeks in the year, it is clear that they did not go home on vacation. At Christmas, Lady Day, Midsummer and Michaelmas they were sent new clothes–cap, shirt, doublet, nether-stocks, gown; all these and other items (e.g. cost of candles, paper, mending of clothes) were studiously recorded by Steward.

The Master of Peterhouse, Andrew Perne, was famous for a career which bore some resemblance to that of Talleyrand two hundred years later. In 1547 he was advocating Catholic doctrine, but recanted shortly afterwards and became royal chaplain at Windsor. On the accession of Mary Tudor he reverted to Catholicism, and was appointed Master of Peterhouse and Dean of Ely. When Elizabeth came to the throne he denounced the Pope and was recommended for a bishopric. 'To perne'– meaning 'to rat' or to change often–was a term coined by his enemies, who also referred to him as 'Andrew Turncoat'; but his abilities were outstanding, and he cannot be dismissed as a crude time-server. The College flourished during his rule, reflecting the versatility of its Master in the variety of its scholars. Here came Jesuits (among them Henry Walpole), and also Puritans, including John Penry, Dudley Fenner and William Brewster.

Campion does not seem to have shown any passion for the religious life and still less for the politics of religion. His mental development must have received more stimulus from the kindred spirits whom he met in Cambridge, but we have little information on this matter. One of his contemporaries at the College was William Percy, probably the same as the author of a sonnet sequence, *Coelia*, to whom Campion addressed an epigram in his book of 1595. Another of his friends, Thomas Nashe, was at Cambridge at the same time and probably knew him there. Christopher Marlowe, who was at Corpus Christi from 1580 to 1586, took a B.A. degree on the same day as Nashe, and collabo- rated with him in the writing of *Dido Queen of Carthage*, but there is no record of any meeting of Campion with Marlowe or with those other University wits, Thomas Kyd and Robert Greene, who were his contemporaries, or with Gabriel Harvey, the Pembroke don who had befriended and influenced Edmund

Spenser when he was a student at the College. Robert Greene[1] spoke of his own life at the University after graduating as 'spent among wags as lewd as myself, with whom I consumed the flower of my youth'. But from various accounts we know that the undergraduate's life was monastic, his work day beginning at 4 or 5 o'clock in the morning with prayer, followed by an 'exhortation' and studies until 10 o'clock at night.[2]

In spite of the turbulent changes that had come and the new conflicts and excitements all over Europe, Oxford and Cambridge kept up their mediaeval tradition and a curriculum designed largely to ensure a supply of educated churchmen. Students were required to behave accordingly and to wear 'sad colours' at a time when the Court was parading peacock finery. Evidently the students were tempted to follow this example, for the Chancellor, Lord Burleigh, issued proclamations against these vices, and particularly against the wearing of hats. There were, nevertheless, relaxations, including tennis and football, music and plays. Music was also a subject in which the University conferred degrees, Robert Fayrfax, John Bull and Orlando Gibbons being among the illustrious graduates in music.

In April 1586, at the age of nineteen, Thomas Campion was admitted to Gray's Inn. Law must have seemed the obvious career for him, and Gray's Inn belonged to what was perhaps the best legal university in Europe. At a time when Oxford and Cambridge were living in the past, these law schools of London were occupying something like the position which Oxford and Cambridge came to occupy later. Fortescue described the Inns of Court as

> a sort of academy or gymnasium fit for persons of their station, where they learn all kinds of music, dancing and other such accomplishments and diversions which are suitable for their quality and such as are usually practised at Court. At other times, out of term [he continues], the greater part apply themselves to the study of law. Upon festival days and after the offices of the Church are over, they employ themselves in the study of sacred and profane

---

[1] Greene's *Groatsworth of Wit*, 1592.

[2] J. H. Ingram, *Christopher Marlowe and his associates*, Grant Richards, London, 1904, p. 67.

history. There everything which is good and virtuous is to be learned, and all vice is discouraged and banished, so that knights, barons and the greatest nobility of the kingdom often place their children in the Inns of Court not so much to make the laws their study, much less to live by the profession, having large patrimonies of their own; but to form their manners and to preserve them from contagion and vice.[1]

At Gray's Inn Campion found an environment which was well suited to his temperament and talents. How much law he picked up is unknown; he was not called to the bar. The other activities of the Inn, however, were much to his taste and gave him the training and the contacts he needed for the development of his poetry, music and masques. Plays and masques were performed at Christmas and on other important occasions before a distinguished audience, and the Queen herself was fond of attending these entertainments. Campion's name appears in the cast of a comedy presented in 1588 before Lord Burleigh, the Earl of Leicester and other noblemen. The play cannot be identified, but it had a Roman subject and included a masque; Campion played the part of Melancholy. At about this time a Senecan tragedy, *The Misfortunes of Arthur*, was written and performed by senior members of Gray's Inn before the Queen at Greenwich. It is not known if Campion took part in it, but he had an opportunity then of meeting Francis Bacon, who appears to have been one of the authors of the tragedy and to have played a minor rôle in its performance. An important occasion which may have brought Campion and Shakespeare together was a performance at Gray's Inn of *A Comedy of Errors* in December 1594. The reference to this event in *Gesta Graiorium* is cursory and the comedy may, in fact, have been one with the same title by another author.[2] We know that his greater comedy of errors, *Twelfth Night*, was played in 1602 at another of the Inns of Court, the Middle Temple.

The Christmas festivities of 1594, when *A Comedy of Errors* was performed, included the traditional 'law sports' at which a student was elected 'Prince of Purpoole' (i.e. Gray's Inn) and for

---

[1] See Mary Sturt, *Francis Bacon*, London, 1932, p. 13.
[2] See *Law Sports at Gray's Inn*, 1594, by Basil Brown, New York, 1921.

some days a programme of entertainments, pageants, proclamations, mock legislation, and ceremonial horseplay was carried
through with great vigour, the whole of it ending with a performance before the Queen of *The Masque of Proteus*. This opens with
Campion's well-known lines 'Of Neptune's Empyre let us sing',
which appear also in Francis Davison's *Poetical Rapsody*. A
sonnet in that miscellany reveals that Davison 'wrote the speech
at Gray's Inn Mask of 1594'; so it appears that Campion and
Davison were collaborators in the entertainment.

By this time Campion was known to *cognoscenti* as a poet. A
pirated edition of Sidney's *Astrophel and Stella* published by
Newman and edited by Thomas Nashe contained 'Poems and
Sonets of Sundry other Noblemen and Gentlemen', among them
being five 'cantos' by Campion. One of them was the song
Harke, al you Ladies which re-appeared with music in Rosseter's
Booke of Ayres. These cantos bore a pseudonym, *Content*; but two
years later George Peele praises Campion by name, and isolated
poems appear in commonplace books as early as 1592. It is clear
that his poems, as Rosseter later remarked, were being 'imparted
privately to friends' and gaining a reputation in this way long
before they were published. His fame as a Latin poet was established through the publication in 1595, by Richard Feild, of
Poemata, a large collection of epigrams, elegies and other poems,
which contains most of his output in this medium. In the same
year William Covell published *Polimanteia*, in which the University of Oxford is praised for the many excellent writers who were
schooled there. It includes the following passage: 'I know Cambridge, howsoever now old, thou hast some young, bid them be
chast, yet suffer them to be wittie; let them be soundly learned,
yet suffer them to be gentlemanlike qualified'; to which there is a
marginal note 'Sweet Master Campion'; a rebuke prompted, no
doubt, by the salacity of some of the epigrams.

In the Latin poems Campion is seen as a man of strong feelings
and varied experience. The names of several friends who were
with him at Gray's Inn—notably the brothers Michelborne,
Francis Manby and James Huish—are mentioned repeatedly and
with affection. The identity of others is concealed (from our eyes,
at all events) by Latin pseudonyms. The women, for example:
the chaste, magnetic Caspia, and the rapacious, inconstant, but
enchanting Mellea; 'divinities who', as Vivian remarks, 'are

depicted in a language and in circumstances that declare them creatures of flesh and blood'. Latin names also hide the real identity of many persons caricatured in his satires.

One of the victims whom we can identify is Barnabe Barnes, a boastful personality paraded by Campion with some relish. Barnes, a close contemporary of Campion and his neighbour in Holborn, achieved fame through the publication in 1593 of *Parthenophil*, a collection of sonnets, madrigals, sestinas, canzones, elegies and odes in many metres. It was an unusual achievement for a youth of twenty-two, both in its technical variety and in being the largest collection of love poems that had yet been published in English. But though it found admirers in its day and contains many lines that are still pleasing, the book is more notable as a treasury of Elizabethan fustian: all the worst faults of bombast and conceit which brought the sonneteers into disrepute are here in profusion. In one sonnet (number 63),[1] for example, the author wishes that he could be dissolved in his mistress' drink, travel by this channel to her heart, and then emerge once more 'through pleasure's part'. Campion's reaction to this fancy is contained in his Latin epigram *In Barnum* (number 17 of Book 1): 'Perhaps you'll reach her heart; but Barnes, what a fine lover you'll be when they fish you out of a chamber-pot!'[2] In the *Observations in the Art of English Poesy* he gives (as a technical example of English trochaic verse) another epigram on Barnes:

> Barnzy stiffly vows that hees no Cuckold,
> Yet the vulgar ev'rywhere salutes him,
> With strange signes of hornes, from ev'ry corner;
> Wheresoere he commes, a sundry Cucco
> Still frequents his eares; yet hees no Cuccold.
> But this Barnzy knowes that his Matilda,
> Skorning him, with Harvy plays the wanton.
> Knowes it? nay desires it, and by prayers
> Dayly begs of heav'n, that it for ever
> May stand firme for him; yet hees no Cuccold.
> And 'tis true, for Harvy keeps Matilda,
> Fosters Barnzy and relieves his houshold,

[1] E. Arber, *An English Garner*, Vol. 5, 1882, p. 377.
[2] *Campion's Works* (ed. Vivian), Oxford, 1909, p. 239.

> Buyes the Cradle, and begets the children,
> Payes the Nurces, ev'ry charge defraying,
> And thus truly playes Matildas husband:
> So that Barnzy now becomes a cypher,
> And himselfe th' adultrer of Matilda.
> Mock not him with hornes, the case is altered;
> Harvy beares the wrong, he proves the Cuccold.

Here, it seems, Campion may have let fancy run away with him, for there is no record that Barnes was ever married; but perhaps the epigram had some symbolic reference to literary politics, especially if, as Vivian thinks, Harvy is Gabriel Harvey.[1] Barnes was ridiculed also by Nashe and by Marston, and Harington summarised his career in a withering epigram:

> Many men marvaile Lynus doth not thrive
> That had more trades than any man alive;
> At first a Broker, then a Petty-fogger,
> A Traveller, a Gamester, and a Cogger,
> A Coyner, a Promoter and a Bawde,
> A spy, a Practicer in every Fraude:
>> And missing thrift by these lewd trades and sinister
>> He takes the best, yet proves the worst, a Minister.

It is clear that before he left Gray's Inn—in 1594 at the earliest —Campion had received an education in life wider than what came his way in that 'gymnasium' of virtuous exercises. Vivian speaks of 'the seductions which Elizabethan London had for a youth of good standing, means and attractive parts', and there is an air of remorse in some of his lines: 'Deceitful Haemus, why do you thrust a defenceless youngster into this town with its dark roads and filthy ways? Here it is easier to go astray than in the labyrinth of Cnossus.'[2] Another kind of experience at which he hints in the Latin poems is warfare. 'It is my luck that I, a lover of peace, should have to endure military service'[3]—that is the gist of his epigram, *De Se*, in the volume of 1595; and in lines addressed to Sir Robert Carey he says 'Once I saw you as you are, in the harsh times when France was raging against herself.'[4] The fighting in question occurred during 1591, when the

[1] *Campion's Works* (ed. Vivian), Oxford, 1909, p. 360.
[2] Ibid., p. 259.   [3] Ibid., p. 345.   [4] Ibid., p. 243.

Earl of Essex led an expedition to help Henri IV of France against the Spanish invaders of Brittany, a small and, for England, futile episode in the long struggle that began with the Armada. On 2nd August the force under Essex arrived at Dieppe and was promptly deployed by the King to lay siege to Rouen, which was in the hands of the League. The siege failed, and Essex was recalled in the following spring. A company of 100 Londoners and 50 Surrey men commanded by Sir Robert Carey went over with the Earl of Essex. By December the company had shrunk to 58, 17 of them sick. Although we have no official record that Campion interrupted his studies at Gray's Inn to go with this expedition, the internal evidence is strong, and it seems likely that he was attached as a 'gentleman adventurer' (or volunteer) to Carey's contingent, returning to England some time before the campaign ended. While abroad, he may have witnessed the killing of the Earl's brother, Walter Devereux, which he describes with vividness and, to judge by the similarity to an account in State papers, with accuracy. It was probably there, too, that he struck up the friendship with Captains Thomas Grimstone and John Goring which he records in another epigram:[1] 'I wonder how things are with our brave Grimstone and Goring in France? None were ever worthier of their pay in wartime, but never has this wretched world paid less respect to courage.'

Another adventurer whom Campion met there (perhaps for the first time) was Barnabe Barnes. So, at least, we gather from Thomas Nashe who regarded Campion as a witness of Barnes's behaviour on the battlefield:[2] 'Having followed the Campe for a week or two . . . to the General he went and told him he did not like of this quarrelling kind of life . . . wherefore hee desired license to depart, for he stood everie houre in feare and dread of his person . . .' Nevertheless on returning to England he boasted of great feats. In a 'universall lauded Latin Poem of Master Campions' Barnes is addressed thus: 'You tell us you killed ten men in combat on the fields of France; but your numbers are wrong. If you were to say you killed no men, Barnes, we should believe you and you would, in fact, be telling the truth.'[3]

[1] Ibid., p. 341.
[2] *Have with you to Saffron Walden.* (See Vivian, op. cit., p. xxxv.)
[3] *Campion's Works* (ed. Vivian), Oxford, 1909, p. 284.

After the scarifying and largely deserved criticism of his earlier morals and writings, it is surprising to find eulogistic verses by Campion, both in English and in Latin, prefixed to Barnes's *Foure Bookes of Offices*, published in 1606.

> Here is the Schoole of *Temperance*, and *Wit*,
> Of *Justice*, and all formes that tend to it;
> Here *Fortitude* doth teach to live and die;
> Then, Reader, love this Booke, or rather buy.

The book, which describes the duties and moral virtues required in a Privy Councillor, a Lord Treasurer, a Judge and a General, was dedicated to King James and had commendatory verses also by John Ford and by Campion's friends William Percy and Thomas Michelborne. Why Campion relented is uncertain. The scoundrel had, apparently, reformed (though he had recently attempted to poison one John Browne, the Recorder for Berwick, and later escaped from prison);[1] he had, at any rate, turned over a new leaf in writing prose rather than sonnets, and this must have seemed like virtue. Even so, Campion did not scrap either of the epigrams to Barnes (as he did some of the others, e.g. *De Se*) when the Latin poems were reprinted in 1619.

We hear no more of Campion at Gray's Inn after 1594. In the eight years that followed he devised and matured the art form which he made his own (words and music of the lute song), and took his place in the musical as well as the literary scene in London. He wrote a dedicatory epigram for Dowland's *First Booke of Songes or Ayres*, published in 1597, comparing Dowland as a musician with Orpheus, a sagacious judgment on the first (or nearly the first) published works of their kind. At this time he must also have become acquainted with Philip Rosseter, the composer who was later his closest friend and with whom he collaborated in the creation of *A Booke of Ayres*, published in 1601. In 1602 he presented his ideas on prosody and on the relationship of words and music in *Observations in the Art of English Poesie*; Daniel's reply to this, with its glimpse of Campion's person and reputation, was published in the same year.

Between this time and the publication of the prefatory verses for Barnes's *Offices* in 1606 we have no word of Campion's

---

[1] M. Eccles, in *Thomas Lodge and other Elizabethans* (ed. C. J. Sisson), Harvard, 1933, p. 167.

Plate 1. Two views of the 16th century hall at Gray's Inn

Plate 2. A Tudor wedding masque

activities in England. He is described in that publication for the
first time as 'Thomas Campion, Doctor in Physick', and it is
reasonable to think that he studied medicine in the period between 1602 and 1606. There is no record that he took a doctorate
in Oxford or Cambridge, the two universities in England which
conferred medical degrees. Peterhouse was, in fact, one of the
headquarters of medical study in England, and Campion's interest
in the subject may have begun while he was there. The College
encouraged students to attend foreign universities, and degrees
in medicine conferred abroad were at that time accepted as a
condition for the practice of medicine in England. It was very
common for English physicians to hold doctorates conferred by
French and Dutch universities, and Vivian considers it likely
that Campion (who refers to the French language and literature
in his epigrams and *Observations*) took a medical degree in France.

In 1932 R. W. Innes Smith[1] published a list of English-
speaking students of medicine at the University of Leyden, and
described in the introduction to his book an account of a more
limited search in some other continental universities, including
Paris, Montpellier, Vaucluse and Caen.

> In the Bibliothèque de la ville de Caen, in Normandy [he
> writes], I found an old manuscript list of promotions at the
> University of Caen. It is incomplete and the calligraphy, in
> particular, beyond me, but I was able to decipher a few
> British and Irish names. Amongst those who are not in the
> Leyden album I found the names of Andrew Balfour (M.D.
> Caen, 1601), Thomas Campion, the poet (M.D. Caen, 10th
> February, 1605) and David Echlin (M.D. Caen, 1613).

This, it seems, may provide the link which Vivian missed. The
University of Caen, founded by Henry VI of England in 1431 –
before he founded Eton College and King's College, Cambridge –
was easy of access and popular with students from England;
something, in fact, of an English university abroad. With its
spires and its mediaeval legacy the city of Caen had much in
common with Oxford and Cambridge, and its population in the
later part of the sixteenth century included a majority of Pro-
testants.

[1] *English-Speaking Students of Medicine at the University of Leyden,*
Edinburgh, 1932.

C

There was an additional factor which may have led Campion
to choose Caen for his studies. Since 1558 the University of Caen
had held every year a poetical contest, the *Concours du Palinod*,
in honour of the Immaculate Conception of the Virgin Mary.[1]
Similar contests were held in the Universities of Rouen, Évreux
and elsewhere, but the *Concours* at Caen achieved considerable
fame in the last quarter of the sixteenth and first quarter of the
seventeenth century because of the remarkable literary talent
shown by competitors. The president for the year was called
Premier Prince du Palinod. On the first day candidates recited
their poems, which were ballades, chants royaux, rondeaux or
Latin epigrams in honour of the Immaculate Conception. On the
second day the judges made their report, and prizes were awarded
for each class of composition, the expenses being met from fines
paid by officials who failed to attend the University congrega-
tions! Among the prizewinners was the poet Malherbe. It is
tempting to think that Campion may have competed with Latin
epigrams at one of the Concours, but there is no record of his
having won a prize.

As a medical school Caen was less outstanding. With the
exception of the great schools of Paris and Montpellier, the
medical faculties of French universities were largely degree-
giving bodies with few teaching facilities. Innes Smith refers to
one John Hustwayt of Hull who took a doctorate of medicine at
Caen on the day after he had qualified as Bachelor and Licentiate.
He then moved to Leyden, which was famous for its medicine,
and applied for permission to receive a doctorate there on the
evidence of his qualification at Caen. Such conferring of degrees
ad eundem was a common practice, but on this occasion the
Faculty decided that a thesis should first be presented.

The music and pageantry of Caen were a feature of the place
that must have appealed to Campion, and he was there during a
high tide of such celebrations. In 1602 there were great rejoicings
in the town at the birth of a son to the King, Henri IV. In the
next year there was a progress of the King through Caen.[2]
Attended by a large company of gentlemen, all mounted on
horses and dressed with great magnificence, he was greeted by
bands of children, by soldiers, by the clergy, by the civic author-

[1] P. Carel, *Histoire de la ville de Caen*, Paris, 1882.
[2] *Ibid.*

ities, by doctors and professors of all faculties in their robes. The streets were carpeted. The King ascended a throne. Musicians played to him on many kinds of instruments and sang *airs de cour*, motets and other pieces specially composed in his honour. There were loyal addresses. Decorations, emblems and inscriptions of Latin verse were hung from the buildings. After divine service, revels continued through the night.

At some time in 1605 Campion, who was nearly forty, began his new career of medicine in London. As physician he practised under licence from the Bishop of London, applying the dogmatic principles handed down by Galen of Pergamum and administering a variety of ineffectual (though, for the most part, harmless) drugs. Luckily for him the terrible epidemic of plague which greeted the accession of James I in 1603 had passed its peak, though it continued its ravages for a number of years, to the discomfiture of the doctors and the delight of quacks. Dekker was harsh but not unfair in his verdict:

> Never let any man ask what became of our phisitions in this Massacre; they hid their synodicall-heads as well as the proudest; and I cannot blame them, for their phlebotomies, losinges and electuaries, with their diacotholicons, diacodions, amulets and antidotes had not so much strength to hold life and soul together as a pot of Pinder's Ale and a Nutmeg. . . . Galen could do no more good than Sir Giles Goosecap.[1]

It is not surprising that Campion's literary output was small during the next five or six years, for medical duties must have exhausted and saddened him. It is more surprising that he managed, in 1607, to produce and publish the first and longest of his masques, for the marriage of Lord Hayes. This entertainment was presented before the King at Whitehall, and the masquers included Lord Walden, Sir Thomas Howard, Sir Henry Carey and other distinguished people. Campion's eminence as a writer had been proclaimed by Camden in 1605, and now his services were wanted by the Court and the nobility. At the same time he was befriended by fellow artists—by John Dowland, Robert Jones, Richard Alison, the younger Ferrabosco, John Cooper ('Coperario') and others who set his words

[1] *Plague Pamphlets* (ed. F. P. Wilson), Oxford, 1925.

as lute songs or madrigals. Prefatory lines by him were an ornament for Ferrabosco's *Ayres*, published in 1609, and for an odd
travel book, *Coryates Crudities hastily gobbled up in Five Months'
Travels in France, Italy, etc.*, published in 1611.

By this time the plague had receded and Campion was at last
given a full opportunity to indulge his creative inclinations. In
1613 he published *Songs of Mourning*, with music by John
Cooper, in memory of Prince Henry, the eldest son of King
James, who had died in the previous year. In the same year he
wrote and published *The Lords' Masque*, for the wedding of the
Princess Elizabeth to the Count Palatine; a *Royal Entertainment*
given by Lord Knowles for the Queen; and the *Masque on St.
Stephen's Night*, presented in the Banqueting Room at Whitehall
on the marriage of Robert Car, the Earl of Somerset, to Frances
Howard. The undated *Two Bookes of Ayres* probably appeared
in this splendidly creative year or shortly afterwards.

On the title-page of these and of later works, Campion is
described as 'Doctor of Physick' or 'Doctor of Medicine' and
there is evidence that he continued to practise. One of his
patients was Sir Thomas Monson, the patron to whom Rosseter
had dedicated their joint publication of 1601. One day in 1613
Sir Gervis Elwes, Lieutenant of the Tower, placed in Campion's
charge the sum of fourteen hundred pounds for the use of Sir
Thomas Monson, who later collected the gold and had the
'white' money fetched by his manservant. How Monson used
this money came out during the investigations which followed
the mysterious death of Sir Thomas Overbury later that year.

Overbury, a courtier and amateur of letters, had for some years
been an inseparable friend of Robert Car, who later became
Lord Rochester and Earl of Somerset. In 1611 it was noticed
at Court that Robert Car and Frances Howard, the Countess of
Essex, were lovers, and later the Countess succeeded in having
her marriage with Essex annulled. Overbury resented the liaison
and warned his friend against a marriage with 'that filthy base
woman'. Car reported these words to Frances Howard and
between them they plotted a revenge that led to the destruction of
Overbury. First Car persuaded Overbury to refuse the post of
Ambassador to Russia which, on Car's recommendation, he had
been offered. For this 'insult' to the King, Overbury was thrown
into the Tower. The next step was to have the Lieutenant of the

Tower, Sir William Wade, replaced by their accomplice, Elwes, who paid two thousand pounds for this arrangement. Sir Thomas Monson negotiated the deal, with Campion acting as receiver. Finally, a new keeper was appointed, Weston by name. Arsenic, blue vitriol, corrosive sublimate and other poisons were brought by Frances Howard's servant, Anne Turner, and administered by Weston to the unfortunate Overbury, who died a slow and painful death. Two months later Car and his lady were married, and Campion's masque was performed in their honour. Then, after a year of rumours, the conspirators were brought to trial. Elwes, Weston and Anne Turner were hanged; Car and Frances Howard were condemned to death, then reprieved and confined for years in the Tower. Campion, when examined, said he had received money from Elwes and handed it to Monson without knowing the reason for this transaction. Monson was kept in the Tower until 1617, when the Court of the King's Bench was satisfied that he had no complicity in the crime and pardoned him. The establishment of Monson's innocence removed any taint that may have fallen on Campion's name.

After these tragic events Campion had three more years of life which were peaceful and productive. *The Third and Fourth Booke of Ayres* appeared probably in 1617, with a dedication to Monson in which he recalls their recent tribulations:

> Since now those clouds, that lately over-cast
> Your Fame and Fortune, are disperst at last . . .
> Shall I but with a common stile salute
> Your new enlargement? or stand onely mute?
> I, to whose trust and care you durst commit
> Your pined health, when Arte despayr'd of it?[1] . . .

In 1618 appeared *Ayres that were sung and played at Brougham Castle* on the occasion of King James's entertainment there by the Earl of Cumberland; the words, probably by Campion, were set to music not by himself but by George Mason and John Earsden. In these later years, however, he was much occupied with ideas on the theory of music and published at about this time *A New Way of Making Fowre Parts in Counterpoint*. For another well-known textbook on music, Ravenscroft's

---

[1] The warrant allowing Campion and another doctor to attend Monson in the Tower is extant (*Campion's Works* (ed. Vivian), Oxford, 1909, p. xlv).

Brief Discourse (1614), Campion wrote a prefatory sonnet. In 1619, returning to his first love, he produced a volume of Latin Epigrams and Elegies in two books, the second being largely a reprint of the volume of 1595. It was to be his last published work. In the same year he wrote a will and a few months later–on 1st March 1620–he died and was buried on the same day at St. Dunstan's in the West, Fleet Street.

We catch a glimpse of the character and personality of Campion in his will. The probate document contains the following sentence:

> Thomas Campion, late of the parishe of St. Dunston's in the West, Doctor of Phisicke, being in perfect mynde and memory, did with an intent to make and declare his last will and testament upon the first of March, 1619, and not longe before his death saie that he did give all that he had unto Mr. Phillip Rosseter, and wished that his estate had bin farr more . . .

It amounted, in fact, to twenty pounds. Friendship seems to have been a dominant emotion of his life. There is no evidence that Campion ever married, and this single-hearted devotion to his fellow artist and compeer is in character. Our other clues about his personality are incidental and fragmentary. From Samuel Daniel, for example, we have it that his appearance was pleasing, but he describes himself as a thin man envious of those better covered (Epigram 23 of Book 2). From a satire, *Of London Physicians*, written in a Cambridge student's commonplace book about 1611, we learn that he was talkative:

> 'How now Doctor Champion, musicks and poesies stout Champion
> Will ye ne'er stop prating?'

We may guess that his conversation, like his writing, was witty as well as erudite and seasoned with irony. He was proud to the point of conceit about his varied gifts: 'Ancient writers say that Apollo practised three arts; all of them I practise too and will always practise; now they all recognise Campion the musician, the poet and the doctor.'[1] With more humility he praises the full yet simple life which one likes to think he enjoyed:

[1] *Campion's Works* (ed. Vivian), Oxford, 1909, p. 259. (*Epigrams*, Bk. 1, 167.)

Thus, scorning all the cares
That fate, or fortune brings,
He makes the heav'n his booke,
His wisedome heev'nly things,

Good thoughts his onely friendes,
His wealth a well-spent age,
The earth his sober Inne,
And quiet Pilgrimage.

3

WORDS FOR MUSIC

THE nature of song is elusive. One is tempted to think of it as a synthesis of components, each incomplete in itself; a union of words and music 'where, for its moment, both seem lost, consumed'. In support of this view it may be said that few (if any) people can accept simultaneously two forms of aesthetic experience involving the same sensory channels, and a poem transmitted and enjoyed through the medium of song cannot at the same time be enjoyed as a poem in its own right. In Valéry's words, 'hearing verse set to music is like looking at a painting through a stained glass window'.[1] In becoming words for music, poetry, complete in its own right, changes its shape and acquires an apparent incompleteness. What then of the music? Does that enjoy an existence independent of the words? If so, does it also sacrifice some of its identity by association with words? Is music the handmaid or the mistress in this clearly uneven relationship? These questions are of peculiar interest in a study of Campion's work as poet-composer, and we shall consider them briefly in this chapter.

It is generally assumed that poetry and music have a common ancestry: or, more precisely, that the first poetry was sung. Orpheus and Arion enchanted their hearers with words sung to the lyre, and at feasts the Epics were transmitted in this way. The rôle of music was subordinate, a background (and perhaps a mnemonic) for the story which was being handed on. In folk-song the words and the music were virtually inseparable; Cecil Sharp[2] notes that singers could not finish a tune if the words failed them, and neither words nor tune could be extracted separately from folk-singers who had always sung both together. Words, again, occupied the chief attention; the tune was sung almost unconsciously, an accompaniment and in that sense sub-

---

[1] See R. W. Ingram, in *Elizabethan Poetry*, Stratford-upon-Avon Studies, No. 2, Edward Arnold Ltd., London, 1960, p. 131.
[2] *English Folk Song: Some Conclusions*, 2nd ed., London, 1936, p. 19.

ordinate, though its aesthetic importance was generally greater than that of the words. Music and verse had quite distinct rôles which did not vie with each other for the listeners' attention.

Bruce Pattison[1] has shown how the two arts were traditionally associated through the centuries, influencing and to some extent dependent upon each other; in the words of Dante, 'vernacular poetry is nothing but a rhetorical composition set to music; neither poetry nor music alone can be called a *canzone*'.[2] This relationship between music and poetry culminated in a great outburst of song during the sixteenth and early seventeenth century, when both arts were passing through a phase of exceptional creative vigour, their mutual regard stimulated by the example of Greece. 'He cometh to you with words set in delightful proportion either accompanied with, or prepared for, the well enchanting skill of music'; that was how Sidney[3] saw the poet's function at the beginning of this period in England. In the seventeenth century new forces drove the sister arts apart, and they evolved on separate lines into forms so independent that a taste for one was seen to be quite compatible with deafness towards the other.

A different view of the relationship of music and poetry is put forward by John Stevens, who considers that Elizabethan vocal writing represents a new phase of improved, though still imperfect, co-operation between the sister arts.[4] He gives examples of the indifference of musicians and poets to each other's achievement in the late Middle Ages and goes on to show how incomplete, in fact, was the 'union' of the arts, at least in the writing of madrigals, during the Elizabethan age itself. This relationship he calls 'an uneasy flirtation' rather than 'a perfect marriage', with music gaining most from the relationship.

It is hard to define this relationship, and some definitions which seem acceptable at first sight cannot stand up to close scrutiny. H. C. Colles,[5] for example, has said that a good song 'heightens through music what the words have to say, the music

[1] *Music and Poetry of the English Renaissance*, Methuen, 1948.

[2] Quoted in Bruce Pattison, op. cit., p. 31 (from *De Vulgari Eloquentia*).

[3] 'An Apology for Poetry', 1595 (in *English Critical Essays* (*Sixteenth, Seventeenth and Eighteenth Centuries*) ed. E. D. Jones, Oxford, 1943).

[4] 'The Elizabethan Madrigal', in *Essays and Studies* (ed. B. Willey) Murray, London, 1958.

[5] H. C. Colles, *Voice and Verse*, London, 1928, p. 9.

giving them some sort of eloquence which they would not have possessed without it'. This may be true of Schubert's settings of Müller, for example, but is it true of his settings of Goethe–or of Quilter's settings of Shakespeare? If a new eloquence is added by the music, it is the eloquence of a different language; not an enhancement, but a concurrent translation.

Another author,[1] regarding song from the angle of literature, accounts for certain qualities in the Elizabethan lyric by suggesting that 'the poetry is waiting for music to give it tone and emphasis'. A similar view was expressed by M. M. Kastendieck,[2] in a study of Campion's work as poet and musician: 'he must be considered a lyric poet in the oldest meaning of the word, that is to say, a musical poet'.[3] Kastendieck argues that the perfect union of words and music results in something which transcends both, the lyric being incomplete without the musical setting. He goes further and argues that the musical rhythm and the verse rhythm are always in agreement, and that the musical setting of a stanza shows how it should be scanned, 'not as accentual verse, but . . . composed quantitatively and rhythmically'[4]; 'since words and notes are coupled lovingly together, any question of scansion is immediately settled by looking at the setting of the air'.[4] The actual quality of the poems is found to be deficient without the music: 'if Campion's lyrics, judged without their musical settings, seem lacking in warmth or are said to be platonically cold, then as a rule the music adds the missing quality.'[5] As regards the music, Schubert's melodies are self-sufficient, but Campion's are 'merely melodic outlines'.

The inference that must be drawn from this *reductio ad absurdum* is that the music and poetry of Campion's songs considered in themselves are deficient. But poems which are ranked with the best lyrics in the language cannot be dislodged in this way. In his effort to produce a 'monistic' account of Campion's art, Kastendieck gives the best evidence to refute his own theory; and it is obvious that while the scansion of the words is perfectly matched by the music, the words when read without the music often have quite a different scansion (see pp. 36–37).

A more realistic view of the marriage of words and music in

[1] Hallett Smith, *Elizabethan Poetry*, Harvard University Press, 1952, p. 268.
[2] *England's Musical Poet: Thomas Campion*, New York, O.U.P., 1938.
[3] Ibid., p. 47.   [4] Ibid., p. 131.   [5] Ibid., p. 143.

song is that the simultaneous impact of the two media gives an experience which is not necessarily more intense or more complete than either medium experienced by itself, but by its nature different. There is an added dimension, an extra level of sensation, a holding of our attention concurrently on more than one level; but there is also a loss in the appreciation of the poem as a poem. Many lyrical poems (probably most of those by Campion) were, admittedly, written for music, and their metrical design and language were to some extent determined by this fact. But it seems unlikely that the poet, even if he was also the composer, had a tune foremost in his mind while writing the words; if he did, it is surprising that the words often have an independent metrical design quite different from that which they assume in their musical setting.

At first sight the function of song seems to be communication of what the words already convey. The inadequacy of this view is shown up by the intense satisfaction one may have in hearing a song with words in an unknown language. Hugo Wolf would only set poems that moved him, and did so with meticulous care for the words. But the words were to him a necessary catalyst or stimulus to composition rather than a framework without which the finished music would collapse. Other composers have not required the stimulus of good poetry, and some have even made enjoyable songs out of catchwords, slogans and lists (Gibbons' *Cries of London*, for example, or Henry Lawes' setting of a table of contents—which, incidentally, proved the point he intended to ridicule). What elevates the setting of good poetry above that of doggerel is the subtlety, truth and interest of the subject matter, and this is to the poem, more or less, what the words are to the song—a part, but not the most essential part, of the form.

But while good music loses little or none of its goodness by association with indifferent poetry, no degree of excellence in a poem can make us enjoy an indifferent musical setting of it; indeed the better the poem, the less we can endure such a setting. Song may be a vehicle for the expression of verbal communication, but clearly it is this vehicle that makes the song. We can only see what the words really amount to as poetry by reading them separately and hearing their own music, which is something quite independent.

Let us consider an example, the first stanza of the eleventh song in Rosseter's *Booke of Ayres*, Part I, by Campion. Here are the words:

> Faire, if you expect admiring,
> Sweet, if you provoke desiring,
> Grace deere love with kind requiting.
> Fond, but if thy sight be blindnes,
> False, if thou affect unkindnes,
> Flie both love and loves delighting.
> Then when hope is lost and love is scorned,
> Ile bury my desires, and quench the fires
> > that ever yet in vaine have burned.

And here is Campion's setting of his poem (with the original barring and the lute part literally transcribed in modern notation):

bury my desires, and quench the fires that ev-er yet in vaine have burn-ed.

It is clear that we can learn nothing about the prosody of this poem from the tune. The first six lines are accentual trochaic tetrameters (like the lines in which Ceres and Juno bless the lovers in Act IV, scene 1 of *The Tempest*), and these are followed by a trochaic pentameter and a rambling iambic line of nineteen syllables. The poem has charm, but hardly ranks with the best of Campion. The musical setting, however, has a translucent vividness and magic, the secret of which lies largely in the descending phrase of longer notes on the words 'grace deere love', with its striking effect of false relation in the accompaniment, F♮ being almost immediately contradicted by F♯. Such an effect is unimaginable in the spoken poem. In the poem, however, we can savour subtleties of internal rhyme and the less obvious thoughts that pass unnoticed when we hear the words sung. A more striking example of the independence of song and poem is Rosseter's *When Laura Smiles*, one of the most original and enchanting of all the lute songs, but with words that are little better than doggerel. At the other extreme are a few songs from the later books of Campion (e.g. *The Man of Life Upright*) in which good poems are mated to square, unmemorable tunes.

Unless the poem and the song are considered as separate works of art, one is easily lured to some improbable viewpoints. Mr. Hallett Smith, for example, seems to imply that the rhythmic subtleties of Byrd's madrigal *Though Amaryllis dance in green* are features of the poem which can be appreciated only through a knowledge of the music.[1] But these subtleties are essentially features of the music: the rhythms of the poem are simple and unsubtle.

The tunes of many lute songs can, like their poems, stand by

---

[1] Hallett Smith, op. cit., p. 263.

themselves without the words, as some of them do in the Fitz-william Virginal Book (e.g. Dowland's *Lachrimae* and Campion's *Faine would I wed a faire yong man*). But the music is the same, whether it is accompanied by words or played by an instrument; the duality of poem and song is not paralleled by a similar duality of tune and song. At most we can say, with Morley, 'singing only the bare note, as it were a music made only for instruments . . . will indeed show the nature of the music but never carry the spirit and, as it were, the lively soul which the ditty giveth'.[1]

While it is important in the study of song to stress the independence of poetry and music, the influence of the arts upon each other is clearly a matter of great interest. In strophic songs, for example, the choice of words and images in successive stanzas must match the recurrence of the same musical phrases. Such a discipline, in addition to that required for the production of good rhyming verse, might be expected to limit the variety and vitality of word music. A more obvious influence is that of the events, images and emotions expressed in the poems on the musical form created for them. No body of work is more instructive about such influences than the song books of Campion in which (to quote him) 'I have chiefly aymed to couple my words and notes lovingly together'.[2]

It is significant that Campion used the lute song rather than the madrigal for setting his poems. Both forms were at the peak of their fashion and development during Campion's creative life; but while the madrigal was a predominantly polyphonic form in which several voices carried the words through an often complex web of imitation, the lute song was predominantly homophonic, a melody with accompaniment. The words fitted to the melody were at the focus of attention and could be clearly understood, in contrast with the overlapping and repetitious phrases that commonly appeared in the madrigal. 'To sing to the lute', said Castiglione in *The Courtier*, 'is much better [than counterpoint], because all the sweetness consisteth in one alone, and a man is more heedfull and understandeth the feate manner, the aire or vaine of it, when the eares are not busied in hearing any more

---

[1] *A Plain and Easy Introduction to Practical Music* (ed. Harman), Dent, 1952, p. 293.
[2] *Campion's Works* (ed. Vivian), Oxford, 1909, p. 115.

than one voice.'[1] Although the composers of polyphony often
took great pains to represent every nuance of emotion or action
described in the text with appropriate illustrative music, they
reflected the subject matter rather than the actual phrases of the
poem. It is therefore not surprising that there is a larger proportion of good poetry in the song books than in the madrigal
collections.

A tradition had sprung up in France which gave poets a certain
dominance in their partnership with composers. At the Académie
de Poésie et de Musique which was founded in 1570 by Baïf, one
of the leaders of the Pléiade, it was taught that the long and short
syllables of verse should be set to notes of corresponding value
(*musique mesurée*). The poets, in their turn, were recommended
by Ronsard to make their verses fit the musical setting. The
application of these principles–as, for example, in the songs of
Claude le Jeune (1528–1600) and Eustache du Caurroy (1549–
1609)–made for homophonic, chordal texture. When the English
lute song made its debut in 1597 with Dowland's first book of
Airs, the musical idiom was already well established in Europe–
Luis Milán's songs accompanied by the vihuela (a Spanish relative of the lute) were published as early as 1536. The English
composers were familiar with this background, and also with the
literary idea of the Pléiade which possibly influenced them
towards a meticulous treatment of words; on one occasion Campion actually tried (with little success) to adopt the strict formula
of *musique mesurée* (see p. 57 and p. 72).

The lute song– part of a much greater musical flowering–
began and ended at about the same time as the English schools
of madrigal and virginal music. Some composers, such as Robert
Jones and Thomas Morley, turned their hands to madrigal as
well as lute song, but most were specialists–Dowland, Daniel,
Campion and Rosseter, for example, in lute song, and Wilbye,
Weelkes and Gibbons in madrigal. Between 1597 and 1612 there
was a remarkable flow of lute song publications: in addition to
those we have mentioned, there were books by Michael Cavendish, Thomas Ford, Thomas Greaves, Tobias Hume, William
Corkine, John Cooper (or 'Coperario'), Francis Pilkington,
George Mason and John Earsden. After 1612 the tempo of lute

---

[1] *The Courtier*, by B. Castiglione (transl. Hoby, 1561), David Nutt,
London, 1900, p. 118.

I.

Vthor of light reuiue my dy- ing spright, Redeeme it from the snares of all con- foun-ding night. Lord,light me to thy blessed way:For blinde,for blinde with worldly vaine de- sires, I wander as a stray: Sunne and Moone,Starres and vnderlights I see, But all their glorious beames are mists and darknesse being compar'd to thee.

1 Author of light reuiue my dying spright,
Redeeme it from the snares of all-confounding night.
        Lord,light me to thy blessed way :
For blinde with worldly vaine desires I wander as a stray.
        Sunne and Moone, Starres and vnderlights I see,
. But all their glorious beames are mists and darknes being compar'd to thee.

2 Fountaine of health my soules deepe wounds recure,
Sweet showres of pitty raine, wash my vncleannesse pure.
        One drop of thy desired grace
The faint and fading hart can raise, and in ioyes bosome place.
        Sinne and Death, Hell and tempting Fiends may rage;
But God his owne will guard,and their sharp paines and griefe in time asswage.

Fig. 1. A song by Campion from the *First Booke of Ayres*

ALTVS.

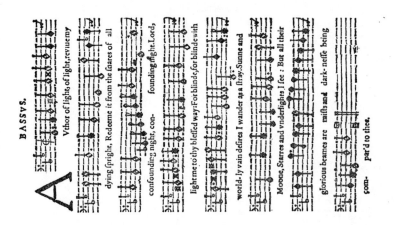

BASSVS.

TENOR.

song production slowed down. Few song books were published and none by a newcomer until 1620, when Martin Peerson offered his *Private Musicke*, a book which departed from convention in having no lute tablature,[1] and in recommending the singer to use viols, lute or virginal for accompaniment. In John Attey's first and only book of airs (1622) there was a return to the traditional genre of Dowland, but it was the last publication of its kind. After this the Italian monodic style of Caccini, d'India and Monteverdi became fashionable. Walter Porter's *Madrigals and Airs* (1632) were written in this style; another well-known example is the anonymous setting of Ben Jonson's stanza *Have you seen but a white lily grow*, and there are manuscripts of Campion's poems recast in this manner with florid embellishments to meet the new taste.

Lute songs were published in folio volumes, generally with the melody and lute tablature on the left side; supporting vocal parts were often printed and arranged on the pages so that singers could stand around and read their parts (see Figure 1). Voice and lute are kept together by bar-lines, which do not necessarily imply 'strong' beats, and whose position is often irregular; in one of Dowland's songs, for example, a bar of fourteen beats follows one of four. In most of the songs, and especially in those based on the simpler dance or folk-song rhythms, the accentuation of the music is implicit in the rhythmic pattern, and aided by the position of dissonance and the accentuation of the words. In modern editions many of the songs have been re-barred to simplify interpretation: irregularities of bar length, however, are often retained, and these give some visual impression of the sudden changes of rhythm so characteristic of Elizabethan music.

Gustave Reese has said of the lute songs in general that they were written with a nice concern for form, balance and elegance of expression, and usually–like the contemporary madrigal and lyric poetry in England–without much display of personal and romantic feelings. The exceptions, in his view, are Dowland and, occasionally, Campion whose music 'is tinged with an intensity of emotion that reminds one of Gesualdo and Monteverdi'.[2] The sad and serious airs in which Dowland excelled often have

[1] The notation for the lute; it indicated the strings and frets on which the fingers were to be placed to produce the notes.

[2] *Music in the Renaissance*, 1954, p. 838.

broad asymmetrical phrases based on speech melody; many of them have elaborate lute accompaniments, and some are 'durch-komponiert' or written in two or three sections. The lighter songs are generally strophic, chordal and full of rhythmic subtlety. The harmonic idiom of these songs is transitional, and shows the emergence of major and minor keys as we know them today, side by side with a survival of modal features.

In their setting of poetry the lutenist song-writers achieved excellence by following the words truthfully but not slavishly. Morley stressed the importance of providing music appropriate in texture, rhythm and movement to the subject matter, and advised the composer to respect the poet's quantity and accent: 'we cause no syllable which is by nature short be expressed by many notes or one long note, nor no long syllables be expressed with a short note'.[1] But Morley had in mind particularly the madrigalian forms, of which Campion said that they are 'long, intricate, bated with fuge, chaind with sincopation, and where the nature of everie word is precisely exprest in the Note, like the old exploided action in Comedies, when if they did pronounce *Memeni*, they would point to the hinder part of their heads, if *video*, put their finger in their eye'.[2] Though they let the words speak clearly and with a minimum of distortion, the lute song writers allowed themselves more liberty, and were capable of such inconsistencies as pronouncing the word *deceive* with emphasis on the first syllable in one song and on the second in another.

Surprisingly, this particular example is from Campion.[3] It might be supposed that the accentual conventions of Jacobean English, like its spelling, were fluid enough to allow such alternative pronunciations; but Campion himself disarms this line of argument by telling us, in the *Observations in the Art of English Poesie*, that 'in words of two sillables, if the last have a full and rising accent . . ., the first sillable is always short, unlesse position or the diphthong doth make it long; as *desire, preserve, define* . . .'.[4] It seems that the composer (and in this instance the poet too) saw good reasons for a small departure from the normal pronunciation

[1] *A Plain and Easy Introduction to Practical Music* (ed. Harman), Dent, 1952, p. 291.
[2] *Campion's Works* (ed. Vivian), Oxford, 1909, p. lxviii.
[3] See Rosseter's *Booke of Ayres*, I, No. 8, and *Third Booke of Ayres*, No. 26.
[4] *Campion's Works* (ed. Vivian), Oxford, 1909, p. 54.

which *in the song* is aesthetically unimportant. Milton would, undoubtedly, have considered this an outrage to the poetry described. He said of Henry Lawes that he

> First taught our English music how to span
> Words with just note and accent, not to scan
> With Midas' ear, committing short and long.

It seems unlikely that the songs of Dowland, Campion and Robert Jones were unknown to the musical son of a composer represented in *The Triumphs of Oriana*; yet Milton addresses Lawes (in whom Warlock saw 'the great tradition in its decadence and decay') as

> the man
> That with smooth air couldst humour best our tongue.

Much of the poetry in the lute song books can be enjoyed for its own sake, and some of it ranks with the finest lyric verse in the language. The level is most consistently high in the books of Campion, but others–notably those of Dowland, Daniel, Hume, Ford, Jones and Ferrabosco–have many excellences. Some of the best poetry is anonymous (e.g. *Fain would I change that note* and *I saw my lady weep*); but there are also many good poems of known authorship. Sidney's words were used by Jones, Corkine and Robert Dowland; John Dowland and Cavendish set Fulke Greville; Ferrabosco set Donne and Ben Jonson; and Attey, looking back, set Sir Thomas Wyatt; Campion's poems were set by John Dowland, Robert Jones, Ferrabosco and others. Some of the verse is slight (e.g. Hume's hunting and tobacco trivialities), and some is undoubtedly poor; among the latter, surprisingly, much of the text used so well by Philip Rosseter, of which we shall have more to say in the next chapter.

In structure, the song poems are usually simple and strophic, with great variety of rhyme scheme and stanza form, but more conformity of rhythm. Although stanzas were the rule, there are many exceptions, including sonnets set by Daniel and by Dowland. The poems are, for the most part, written in the Petrarchan tradition and concerned with love, especially rejected love; with the transience of life; with Time and Change; and a few with God and Eternity. Some are profound and deeply felt, others light and radiant; others, again, bristling with nonsense, mischief, salacity and high spirits. One feature most commonly found in the lightest as well as the more serious poems is a use or a show of argument; and if we are to name one thing in which, on the whole, they are deficient it is word-painting. Abstractions are frequent and (particularly in Campion) references to music.

Another characteristic (we would scarcely call it a deficiency) is the absence—in the poetry as in the music—of pronounced individual styles such as we find particularly in the work of nineteenth- and twentieth-century artists. The artistic conscience of Elizabethans, on the other hand, was concerned with observing the code of behaviour known from antiquity as rhetoric and acceptable to the Elizabethan temperament as one of its keys to the world of Order. In addition to rhyme, metre, metaphor and other ornaments, there was a range of rhetorical devices which had the effect of blunting the individual voice. Differences of style can, of course, be seen, especially in the work of the greatest poets; but some of these differences (e.g. between the work of Raleigh and Sidney) reflect the cleavage between the older style (what C. S. Lewis has called 'drab') and the richer ornamental ('golden') style which came into flower with Spenser's *Shepheard's Calendar* (1580).

Perhaps for this reason it has been said that the poems are without true personal feeling. Agnes M. C. Latham, for instance, puts it thus:

> The typical Elizabethan poem contains no jot of personal emotion . . . it is baffling and beautiful: baffling because it is beautiful and nothing else. Thought is not permitted to distort it, nor feeling to betray it into incoherencies.[1]

This is surely looking at the Elizabethan world through nineteenth-century spectacles. It is irrelevant to ask whether the poet is telling his true life story or confabulating; what is essential is that he should give us the sense of authenticity, and we find this in the best Elizabethan poetry. If his song of despair and misprized love moves us, then we cannot label the poet as dispassionate.

Catherine Ing,[2] in her study of Elizabethan lyrics, comments on the public and generalised qualities of poems which are

[1] *The Poems of Sir Walter Ralegh*, London, 1929, p. 13.
[2] *Elizabethan Lyrics*, Chatto & Windus, 1951, p. 15.

particularly suitable for singing, and adds that 'the subject of the poem, whether emotion or situation giving rise to emotion, must be freed from those elements which might connect it so intimately with an individual human personality that his privacy might be invaded by the overhearing of his utterance'. And yet the situations expressed in songs like Dowland's *In darkness let me dwell* or Campion's *The Sypres curten of the night is spread* are not greatly different from those expressed in the tragic, personal poems of Müller and of Heine that Schubert and Schumann set. Some of the impersonality that twentieth-century readers see in Elizabethan poetry is probably due to archaisms that give a formal, statuesque air to quite informal statements. In all genuine poetry, however, there is an element of abstraction, and the situation described in the poem of Wolf's *Verborgenheit*, no less than in the poem of Dowland's *Flow my tears*, is both private and universal.

ROSSETER'S BOOK OF AIRS

THERE is no mention of Campion on the title-page of *A Booke of Ayres* (1601), which contains much of his best music and some of his finest poems. That is presumably what Campion wanted,[1] for his participation in the joint venture with Philip Rosseter is apologetic. While Rosseter's name appears in full over the list of his songs, Campion's set is headed 'by T. C.'; and following Rosseter's signed dedication of the book to Sir Thomas Monson there is an address *To the Reader* which is unsigned but rather obviously the work of Campion. Monson's Coat of Arms is printed on the reverse of the title-page, and Rosseter commends the book to his patron with a reference to the many favours which 'Master Campion' had received from him, pointing out that the contents of the first set were by Campion,

> made at his vacant houres and privately emparted to his friends, whereby they grew both publicke and (as coine crackt in exchange) corrupted . . . in regard of which wronges, though his selfe neglects these light fruits as superfluous blossomes of his deeper studies, yet hath it pleased him upon my entreaty, to grant me the impression of part of them, to which I have added an equall number of mine owne. . . .

The address *To the Reader* is almost a breviary of the musical and poetic beliefs (and contradictions) which are fully expounded in Campion's two treatises. The following extract on the Air is interesting too, as a statement about the kinds of song which the artist intends to give us:

> What Epigrams are in Poetrie, the same are Ayres in musicke, then in their chiefe perfection when they are short

---

[1] If Campion's name was associated with the expedition under the Earl of Essex in 1591, he may have wished to avoid publicity in 1601, the year of the rebellion and execution of Essex (see pages 22–3).

and well seasoned . . . Manie rests in Musicke were invented
either for necessitie of the fuge, or granted as an harmonicall
licence in songs of many parts: but in Ayres I find no use
they have, unlesse it be to make a vulgar and triviall modulation seeme to the ignorant strange, and to the judiciall
tedious. A naked Ayre without guide, or prop, or colour but
his owne, is easily censured of everie eare, and requires so
much the more invention to make it please. . . . The lyricke
poets among the Greekes and Latines were the first inven-
ters of Ayres, tying themselves strictly to the number, and
value of their sillables, of which sort you shall find here
onely one song in Saphicke verse; the rest are after the
fascion of the time, eare-pleasing rimes without Arte . . .

This is characteristic of Campion—the emphasis on homo-
phony, the comparison of airs with epigrams, and the gay
unconcern with which he praises the Air for its classic qualities
and then proceeds to offer 'eare-pleasing rimes without Arte'. But
art of a rare and classic simplicity they certainly show, whether
we regard them as poems or as songs.

The Poems of Part I

The metrical and strophic design of these poems is extremely
varied; indeed, there are only two which are cast in the same form.
It seems likely that the construction of the poems, as well as the
arrangement of contents, was devised with at least half an eye to
musical setting, but their poetic effectiveness cannot be regarded
as a fortuitous by-product. It is clear that Campion thought
independently of the poetic and the musical elements, and when
the two elements do not combine successfully, it is usually the
claims of poetry that triumph.

The subject of the poems is mostly amorous, but again with
great variety of attitude, in some poems contented, in some
sensuous, and in some despairing. There is a variety of expostulation, meditation and narrative. The speaker is sometimes a man
and sometimes a woman. Although there is plentiful use of the
conceits and figures which were part of the language of poetry
in the 'Golden' period, these are not used with the careless
abandon that makes so much of the Elizabethan sonnet literature
trite and dull. There is, in addition to variety of form and content,

a sparkle and sophistication, an ironic objectivity at times, which suggest the epigrammatist more than the lyrist, and his fusion of these elements with an intensity of passion sometimes calls to mind the metaphysicals rather than the sonneteers.

The poems have the air of a sequence. This is due not to any continuous thread of story or argument, but to the way in which successive poems are sometimes connected by some word or image or idea (e.g. numbers 11, 12 and 13), and also to the subtleties of contrast and imitation. The sequence is knit to-gether by features of style–an unemphatic and quiet word music, an imagery which is equally unemphatic–at least in its visual aspects, and a nice integration of the particular and the general; qualities which also make the poems ideally suited to musical setting.

The first poem is a variation on Catullus' *Vivamus, mea Lesbia.* An anonymous version similar to this one (possibly a corruption of it) appears in Corkine's *Second Booke of Ayres,* and the same subject was used by Ben Jonson in *Volpone* (Act III, scene 6). Jonson's treatment of this favourite theme is simple and direct, technically flawless but with few surprises:

> Come, my Celia, let us prove
> While we can the sports of love.
> Time will not be ours for ever,
> He at length our good will sever;
> Spend not then his gifts in vain;
> Suns that set may rise again;
> But if once we lose this light,
> Tis with us perpetual night . . .

For the rest, "tis no sin love's fruits to steal', provided we keep quiet about it.

Campion's version is quite different and quite characteristic of his style. There are three stanzas, the first putting forward the conventional idea which forms the body of Jonson's poem:

> My sweetest Lesbia, let us live and love,
> And though the sager sort our deedes reprove,
> Let us not way them; heav'ns great lampes doe dive
> Into their west, and strait againe revive.
> But soone as once set is our little light,
> Then must we sleepe one ever-during night!

In the second stanza he argues that wars would cease if all would
love as he does, and in the last he invites his friends to enjoy
'sweet pastimes' at his funeral, for death when it comes will be
'timely' and no cause for sorrow. The poem is in undertones.
References to love are in cool, contented language, with a recurrence of the key word 'little' in the penultimate line of each
stanza. The stanzas seem to echo the cycles of day and night
described in the poem. In the words of C. S. Lewis, 'the poignancy of "soles occidere et redire possunt" vanishes into the vast
image of "heav'ns great lampes doe dive Into their west, and
strait againe revive." The speed, the brilliance of their movements
is what impresses us; we want to applaud rather than to weep.
. . . Something sunny like Ronsard and gentle like Tibullus has
dissipated the passion.' It is so calm and so apparently logical
that we are lulled into accepting the *reductio ad absurdum* of a
'happie tombe' and a world where all is love and harmony.
Neither the music nor Campion's theories of metre throw any
light on the metrical pattern of such poems as this one; fortunately the metre is clear enough to need no further explana-
tion.

The next poem, *Though you are yoong and I am olde*, is akin to
the first in presenting an unusual idea in very simple language;
the gist of it is contained in the following couplet:

> You are more fresh and faire than I,
> Yet stubs do live when flowers doe die.

Like a ghostly echo of the first poem, it refers to death in the last
line of each stanza; but the theme re-emerges in the minor key
with a strange mixture of pathos and callousness:

> Thinke that thy fortune still doth crie,
> Thou foole, to-morrow thou must die.

In the third poem we are back to the spirit of the first, but
with a dancing rhythm and with a swagger that derives something, perhaps, from the argument of the second poem. It is like
a dance, with its lightness, gaiety, formalities of rejection and
acceptance, and a refrain of four lines; at the same time it is a
teasing criticism of the divinities to whom many of the poems are
addressed:

> If I love Amarillis
> She gives me fruits and flowers,
> But if we love these Ladies
> We must give golden showers:
> Give them gold that sell love,
> Give me the Nutbrowne lasse,
>> Who when we court and kiss,
>> She cries, forsooth, let go.
>> But when we come where comfort is,
>> She never will say no.

After this comes the famous *Followe thy faire sunne, unhappy shadowe*. Here we have the divinity herself, of whom he is the poor shadow, but in Campion's chameleon vein the image keeps changing; he is dark because she deprives him of light; he is dark because she has scorched him; and then (with a backward glance at the second poem)

> There comes a luckles night,
> That will dim all her light.

But this time he says

> Follow still since so thy fates ordained;
>> The Sunne must have his shade,
>> Till both at once doe fade,
> The Sun still proud, the shadow still disdained.'

According to Kastendieck the musical setting of this poem shows that it is not scanned in the way we would read it, viz. (to borrow quantitative language) a trochaic pentameter, two iambic trimeters and an iambic pentameter. But the error of the 'unitarian' view can be shown by reading the poems aloud with the stresses (and, presumably, the repeated words) of the setting. The metrical pattern is, in fact, quite straightforward. The 'abba' rhyme scheme matches the regular alternation of two long and two short lines. The stanzas do not have the same end line, but a similar effect is achieved by the use of the word 'follow' at the beginning of each stanza. The recurrence of identical rhythms in the corresponding lines of each stanza, which is required by the music, is an ornament also for the poem, particularly apparent when, as here, the lines are of varying length.

The next poem (*My love hath vowd hee will forsake mee*) is, in a sense, complementary to the carefree dance-song (Number 3) on the 'wanton countrey maide'; this is the woman's cry of remorse after betrayal. The content is conventional, the language simple and song-like, with a refrain ('I will go no more a-maying') that comes fully to life in the song setting. Both this and the next poem (*When to her lute Corrina sings*) are made memorable by the music and hard to conceive as poems in their own right once we have the songs by heart. The latter poem, however, has great vitality of phrase (e.g. 'As any challeng'd eccho cleere', and 'my thoughts enjoy a sodaine spring'); like many other lyrics of Campion, it makes effective play with the contrasted moods of light and darkness, life and death.

The seventh poem (*Turne backe, you wanton flyer*) is less successful. Quiller-Couch tried to improve it by altering the arrangement of lines, which are distractingly irregular; and Bullen substituted the word 'swerving' for 'changing' in the following lines:

> There's no strickt observing
> Of times or seasons changing;

but although this repairs an unhappy breach in the rhyme scheme, it offends the ear with its clash of s's, and the meaning of 'swerve' in this context is eccentric (contrast its use in 1, 15). Campion was evidently unhappy about the poem; although he liked the section beginning 'What harvest halfe so sweete is' well enough to reproduce it in the *Second Booke of Ayres* (No. 10), the second version is revised and the irregularities of the first version are smoothed out.

The eighth poem strikes a new note of playful and sensuous word magic. Beginning with a phrase that recalls so many folk songs, it turns into a very different kind of narrative:

> It fell on a sommers day,
> While sweete Bessie sleeping laie
> In her bowre, on her bed,
> Light with curtaines shadowed,
> Jamy came: shee him spies,
> Opning halfe her heavie eies.

The words are simple, and there is hardly a stress on any syllable. This conveys the feeling of a breathless summer haze through which 'she heard him, yet would not heare'. The risk of monotony is avoided by the stresses and caesuras of the third and fifth lines of the stanzas. Drawn into the trance (as in *My sweetest Lesbia*) we suffer no jar from the playful irony with which the last stanza closes:

> And since this traunce begoon,
> She sleepes ev'rie afternoone.

The poem which follows this exquisite trifle is also about sleep, but in other respects as different as could be. There are three stanzas of six lines:

> The Sypres curten of the night is spread,
> And over all a silent dewe is cast.
> The weaker cares by sleepe are conquered;
> But I alone, with hidious griefe, agast,
> In spite of Morpheus charmes, a watch doe keepe
> Over mine eies, to banish carelesse sleepe.

The nightmare grows in the two stanzas that follow. A ghost, he sees the map of hell; all hopes are cast out; he implores Griefe to seize his soul 'for that will still endure', and will prove a tastier morsel than all the thousand souls upon which he is already feasting. The metaphysical extravagance of this–characteristically framed in calm, symmetrical verse–takes us back in spirit to *Followe thy faire sunne*; but while the reason for his grief and distraction is explicit in the earlier poem, it is unexplained in the later. Like Gerard Hopkins' last sonnets, the poem may gain something from this omission, by which it escapes the risk of sentimental exaggeration. In spite of the deep sorrow which it expresses, the tone is restrained and the sequence of ideas is lively and well-ordered. Its stature as a poem can be tested by comparing it with Dowland's *In darkness let me dwell*, which presents a similar theme, but leaves it undeveloped (except by the music).

The next poem echoes the words and feelings of *Followe thy faire sunne*:

> Follow your Saint, follow with accents sweet;
> Haste you, sad noates, fall at her flying feete:

There is a glancing reference, also, to *Turne backe, you wanton flyer*. Song in this context has attributes of the soul, but is different in some ways; for music is, in effect, the echo of his mistress' beauty—and thus, ironically, the unapproachable divinity scorns what she most resembles. Song, moreover, can evade immortality:

> Then let my Noates pursue her scornfull flight:
> It shall suffice that they were breath'd
>   and dyed for her delight.

The texture is varied and interesting. The natural stress on the fourth syllable of lines 1 and 2 of each stanza, followed by a pause, is effective, and the long end line of each stanza is appropriate to its context of 'bursting with sighs' and 'dying for her delight'.

Poems 11, 12 and 13 form a group. In 11, he addresses her as 'faire' and 'sweet', saying in the first stanza that he will not reward her coldness with love, in the second stanza that if everything else fails he will fly to her again. The twelfth poem (of which there is a sonnet version in manuscript) has almost the same thought structure, but here the lover says 'thou art not faire . . . thou art not sweet . . . unlesse thou pitie mee'; the first stanza ends, as in the eleventh poem, with defiance:

>   thou shalt prove
> That beauty is no beautie without love.

And again in the second stanza, there is the rebound:

> Now shew it, if thou be a woman right,–
> Embrace, and kisse, and love me, in despight.

From which the thirteenth poem takes its theme:

> See where she flies enrag'd from me,
> View her when she intends despite . . .

And again, he is her shadow. Numbers 11 and 13, especially the latter, contain some of Campion's weaker writing, but the consistent use of feminine endings in the eleventh poem is a pleasing feature.

Another group of three, numbers 14, 15 and 16, have as their keynote the name of Cupid. The fourteenth poem, which is structurally the twin of number 12, is particularly fresh. To explain the pallor of his cheeks, he argues that 'The kindly heate' has gone inward to comfort his heart 'that is dismaid by thee'; but those whose cheeks are red (a reference back to the 'rosie ornaments' of number 12) are loveless, and in their breasts

> where love his court should hold,
> Poore Cupid sits and blowes his nailes for cold.

In the next poem Cupid in his cradle inspires his wither'd nurse with fires of love that cannot be quenched; this bagatelle must be read like French poetry, with virtually no stresses if it is to make prosodic sense.

In the sixteenth poem, Campion extends the image:

> Mistris, since you do so much desire
> To know the place of Cupids fire,
> In your faire shrine that flame doth rest,
> Yet never harbourd in your brest . . .
> Even in those starrie pearcing eyes,
> There Cupids sacred fire lyes.

Again the fire is directed outwards, with power to destroy. In the poem that follows, he continues with the same image:

> Your faire lookes enflame my desire:
>   Quench it againe with love.
> Stay, O strive not still to retire:
>   Doe not inhumane prove.

And at last his wishes are granted; time makes amends 'with the revenge of love', and when she leaves him, he calls after her

> till the time gives safer stay,
> O farewell, my lives treasure.

With that farewell we come to the end of the sequence. The four remaining poems are quite separate from each other and only the twentieth has some affinity with the other poems in the book. Number 18, *The man of life upright*, reappears with hardly

a change in *Divine and Morall Songs*, and will be discussed with
the other poems in that book. Number 19 had been printed as a
'canto' in the appendix to Newman's pirated edition (1591) of
Sidney's *Astrophel and Stella*—nine years before the publication
of a *A Midsummer Night's Dream*, parts of which it seems to
anticipate—in the following stanzas for example:

> In Myrtle Arbours on the downes
>   The Fairie Queene Proserpina,
> This night by moone-shine leading merrie rounds
>   Holds a watch with sweet love,
> Downe the dale, up the hill;
>   No plaints or groanes may move
>   Their holy vigill.

It is a hymn in celebration of love, and in execration of those who
reject love. In an acid reference to the *Vigil of Venus* the original
('cras amet qui nunquam amavit, quique amavit nunc amet') is
twisted to a declaration that those who have not loved shall 'lead
Apes in Avernus'—the proverbial fate of old maids.

After this youthful fantasy comes one of Campion's maturest
and most unforgettable poems:

> When thou must home to shades of under ground,
> And there ariv'd a newe admired guest,
> The beauteous spirits do ingirt thee round,
> White Iope, blith Hellen, and the rest,
> To heare the stories of thy finisht love
> From that smoothe toong whose musicke hell can move;
>
> Then wilt thou speake of banqueting delights,
> Of masks and revels which sweete youth did make,
> Of Turnies and great challenges of knights,
> And all these triumphes for thy beauties sake:
> When thou hast told these honours done to thee,
> Then tell, O tell, how thou didst murther me.

The language is direct and unadorned, like that of an observer
whose senses are charmed but whose passions are not involved.
And then, in the last line—with no apparent change of expression
—the smile of content becomes the smile of irony; after the spell
of Ronsard, the shock of Donne. In the last line of Sidney's

With how sad steps, O moon, there is a similar effect. But in Sidney's poem we are prepared for the irony by the context; in Campion's poem we are lulled into expecting anything else. The qualities of the lyrist and the epigrammatist are well integrated in this faultless poem.

What follows (*'Come, let us sound with melodie the praises'*) is a startling anticlimax. In contrast with the previous poem, this piece–the last in Part I–aims at classical form but turns out to be a shapeless rigmarole. It has some relevance, however, to Campion's opinions on prosody, and from this angle we shall return to it in the next chapter.

THE MUSIC OF PART I

Several factors have made it difficult for the value of Campion's music to be fully appreciated today. One factor is, undoubtedly, the diversity of his talents. In contrast with the Renaissance ideal of the balanced man who aspired to do all things well, the ideal cultivated in the nineteenth and twentieth centuries has been specialist and monolithic; hence a distrust of varied talents, of the 'Jack-of-all-trades'. In Campion's case the rediscovered poetry was acclaimed before the music was made available; as a musician he therefore arrived with a handicap, seeming to be more of an amateur than his contemporaries Dowland and Byrd. Moreover, the tension and sophistication of music in our own time is more nearly matched by Dowland's than by Campion's style. Cecil Gray, in 1935, wrote: 'He [Campion] may be conceded to possess a fertile vein of pleasant, but rather undistinguished melody, and that is about all. As a musician pure and simple he is of the second rank.'[1] Diana Poulton, in a quatercentenary broadcast on the music of Campion, took him to task for a lack of dissonance and polyphony and an absence of melismata from his melodic line. But these deficiencies, though true in part–and true especially of the later song books–do not prevent the best of the songs from making a strong aesthetic impact.

Some of the best and most characteristic features in the songs of Campion can be ascribed to his dual rôle of poet-composer. More consistently than any of his contemporaries, Campion weds the music to the words, ensuring as a rule that the melody fits the

[1] *The History of Music*, Kegan Paul, London, 1935.

E

sense of all the stanzas; Dowland, in contrast, seems to have written certain melodies with only the first stanza of the poem in mind. The form evolved by Dowland and Daniel is more complex and foreshadows the art song of the nineteenth century in its harmonic intensity and contrapuntal interest. The lute part is more important in their work; introductory phrases (such as Campion used once only) and short interludes for the lute occur in a number of their songs. Campion's musical gift is essentially that of the melodist, and his success goes further than merely providing suitable vehicles for his poetry; the melodies of his finest songs lose little of their freshness even when sung without the words.

The first part of Rosseter's Book has a larger proportion of good music than the four later books. Only two or three songs in it are of negligible interest, and many of Campion's finest songs are to be found here. Their variety matches that of the poems, and the music, like the poetry, forms an agreeable sequence. All the songs are strophic, and successive stanzas are repeated in exactly the same form. A favourite device of Campion, which he used in all but one of these songs, was to repeat the end of each verse–usually two lines of the poem–with the same music. This can be very effective, and is sometimes functional (as, for example, in *My sweetest Lesbia*, where the repetition emphasises the sense of the last couplet of each stanza, with its reference to 'ever-during night'). Daniel, Rosseter, Jones, Morley, Pilkington and others used this device in some songs, but it is less common in the strophic songs of Dowland.

Campion followed the convention of offering songs (in *Two Bookes of Ayres*) for performance either by voice with instrumental accompaniment, or as part songs (see Figure 1). From a close study of the songs and of the Preface to *Two Bookes of Ayres*, David Greer[1] has put forward the view that most of the airs presented as four-part songs in these books were originally written as part-songs, while most of the three-part settings appear to have been arrangements of airs originally written for solo voice and lute. He also points out that the texture of the three-part settings is often rather sparse, and that Campion clearly regarded the lower voices as optional additions to the lute, not substitutes for it.

[1] 'Campion the Musician', in *Lute Society Journal*, 1967, Vol. IX, p. 7.

MY SWEETEST LESBIA

But soone as once set is our lit-tle light, Then must we sleepe one ev-er-dur-ing night, ev - er - dur-ing night.

2

If all would lead their lives in love like mee,
Then bloudie swords and armour should not be,
No drum nor trumpet peaceful sleepes should move,
Unles alar'me came from the campe of love:
But fooles do live, and wast their little light,
And seeke with paine their ever-during night.

3

When timely death my life and fortune ends,
Let not my hearse be vext with mourning friends,
But let all lovers, rich in triumph come,
And with sweet pastimes grace my happie tombe;
And Lesbia close up thou my little light,
And crowne with love my ever-during night.

The first song, *My sweetest Lesbia* (see pp. 59 and 60), is a perfect introduction to the book and also to Campion's music as a whole. The smooth melodic line with its elusive rhythm has a clarity and freshness to match the words. But in spite of its apparent simplicity, this melody is in fact highly organised, making use of several figures and their inversions:

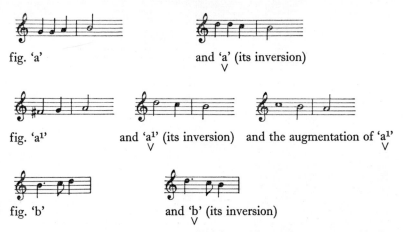

fig. 'a'   and 'a' (its inversion)
                        v

fig. 'a¹'   and 'a¹' (its inversion)   and the augmentation of 'a¹'
                         v   v

fig. 'b'   and 'b' (its inversion)
                        v

A melody lending itself to such detailed analysis is unusual in Campion's work, and it shows a technical maturity which he never surpassed. Features of special interest are the irregular rhythms and the variety of phrase length. In this song, as in many others, Campion's harmony has a modal flavour noticeable particularly in his use of the chord of the flattened seventh. To modern ears this chord has an evocative quality which it probably did not have at a time when it was a normal feature of the musical language. In fact, it is often used by Campion in contexts of strong emotion, sensuousness and strangeness. The music matches the words in its prevailing mood and in various details, such as the longer notes for 'ever-during night', the octave leap to 'heav'ns great lampes', and the musical descent of that lamp 'into its west'. The musical emphasis agrees well with the emphasis required by the words–e.g. on the phrase 'let us live and love'. It is a triumph of strophic form that the same musical phrases should seem appropriate for the contrasted contexts of love and death.

The songs that follow are varied and form a most effective sequence. In the second song *Though you are yoong* (see Figure 2) there is an alternation of tonic minor and relative major which seems to echo the stark contrasts of youth and age, hot and cold, moist and dry, life and death, which are the subject of the poem.

II.

Hough you are yoong and I am olde,

though your vaines hot and my bloud colde, though youth is moist and

age is drie, yet embers liue when flames doe die.

The tender graft is eafely broke,
But who fhall fhake the fturdie Oke?
You are more frefh and faire then I,
Yet ftubs doe liue, when flowers doe die.

Thou that thy youth doeft vainely boaft,
Know buds are fooneft nipt with froft,
Thinke that thy fortune ftill doth crie,
Thou foole to morrow thou muft die.

B 2

Fig. 2. A song by Campion from *A Booke of Ayres.*

The rhythm is simple, and the tune has a haunting quality, with long notes in the vocal line punctuated by more rapid figures for the lute.

After this introspective song, *I care not for these Ladies* has a simple dance-like setting in the major key, with straightforward diatonic harmony except for the flattened seventh on the phrase 'woode and praide'. *Followe thy faire sunne* has a tune which Campion used in a later song (I, 18). Here the words are again lovingly matched with the music, as in the smooth chromatic ascent on 'and she made all of light':

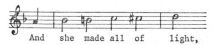

This chromatic phrase transferred to the bass accompanies the lumbering climb of the vocal part for 'yet follow thy faire sun', which reaches its climax on the word 'unhappy':

After this the folk idiom returns, and with no sophistication this time, in the little song of the deserted girl ('*My love hath vowd*' number 5) with its haunting refrain.

One of the most perfect airs of this or any other collection is the sixth, *When to her lute Corrina sings* (see p. 64). Like *My sweetest Lesbia* it has freshness and radiance, and in its general conception and many details it seems like a musical translation of the words. Excellent descriptive touches are the melisma on the words 'revives the leaden stringes', the solo descending phrase for the lute after 'the strings do breake', the octave leap for 'doth in highest noates appeare' and (in the next stanza) 'when of pleasure she doth sing', and the soaring phrase for 'as any challeng'd eccho cleere' and 'my thoughts enjoy a sodaine spring'. There are most effective modulations reflecting the changes of mood in the poem. The brief darkness of the minor opening is dispelled by the sudden radiance of Corrina's voice leading to the relative major in bar 2, while the half-close in G minor which ends the phrase 'but when she doth of mourning speake' suggests the return of clouds passing across the sun.

WHEN TO HER LUTE
CORRINA SINGS

When to her lute Cor - ri - na sings, Her voice re - vives the lead - en stringes, And doth in high - est noates ap-peare, As a - ny chal - leng'd ec - cho cleere; But when she doth of mourn - ing speake, Ev'n with her sighes, her sighes, her sighes, the strings doe breake, the strings doe breake.

2

And as her lute doth live or die,
Led by her passion, so must I,
For when of pleasure she doth sing,
My thoughts enjoy a sodaine spring,
But if she doth of sorrow speake,
Ev'n from my hart the strings doe breake.

The melodic shape of these two phrases, which are similar in
rhythm, has the same symbolism, the second suggesting a dark
reflection of the first. The 'sighes' which follow are reminiscent
of Dowland ('Come again, sweet love', First Book, number 17),
but the song as a whole is most characteristic of Campion.

The next song, *Turne backe, you wanton flyer*, has the idiom of
Campion with little of the magic. Campion may have felt that
his poem deserved better music, for he used the second stanza for
a later setting (II, 10). The overcrowded, dactylic phrases towards
the end of each stanza ('Harts with a thought, Rosie lips with a
kisse') may be due to an attempt to adhere to the principles of
classical quantitative prosody (see Chapter 5).

After this comes another fine song which is at once characteristic of Campion's musical language and unlike anything else
that he wrote (see p. 66). *It fell on a sommers day*—the words and
the tune begin like a folk song, full of innocence and simplicity,
but if we look closely at the four opening bars, we notice something which is far from simple, a passage of double counterpoint
at the 12th between the vocal part and the bass. The first phrase
of the bass is exactly repeated two octaves higher in the voice
part in bars 3 and 4, while the descending vocal phrase in bars
1 and 2 is answered in the following two bars by a similar
descending phrase, with sustained instead of repeated notes in
the bass a twelfth lower. This and other imitative devices (e.g.
bars 5 and 6, and 9 and 10) represent, perhaps, the flight and
pursuit motive underlying the playful deceptions of the poem.
Slight irregularities of rhythm and phrase length, as, for example,
on 'light with curtaines shadowed', or 'opning halfe her heavie
eies', help to evoke an air of siesta, and this is intensified by the
drowsy background of gamba and lute which rises and falls like
the murmur of bees. The interplay of innocence and experience
is paralleled in the mixture of naïvety and sophistication in the

IT FELL ON A SOMMERS DAY

Voice

It fell on a som-mers day, While sweete Bes-sie

Lute

sleep-ing laie In her bowre, on her bed, Light with cur -

-taines sha - dow - ed, Ja - my came:

shee him spies, Op - ning halfe her hea - vie eies.

2

Jamy stole in through the dore,
She lay slumbring as before;
Softly to her he drew neere,
She heard him, yet would not heare,

Bessie vow'd not to speake,
He resolved that dumpe to breake.

3

First a soft kisse he doth take,
She lay still, and would not wake;
Then his hands learn'd to woo,
She dreamp't not what he would doo,
But still slept, while he smild
To see love by sleepe beguild.

4

Jamy then began to play,
Bessie as one buried lay,
Gladly still through this sleight
Deceiv'd in her owne deceit,
And since this traunce begoon,
She sleepes ev'rie afternoone.

musical idiom. The melodic line is full of felicities, and the music matches the words in many details—e.g. the 'caesura' in the middle of the fifth line, and the cadence on the words 'heavie eies' and 'by sleepe beguild'.

After this come several songs on which Campion did not lavish his descriptive powers; the mood of the poem is, to some extent, reflected in the music, but there are fewer imitative devices and less 'translation'. *The Sypres curten of the night* is a song about darkness, fears, griefs, and ghosts. The slow, sustained melody, made up almost entirely of repeated notes or stepwise movement, hovers continually around the opening note:

In the poem a desire to escape from sleep conflicts with a fear of nightmares; this conflict is well expressed by the syncopation (somewhat hidden by Campion's eccentric barring) in the final phrase. The music forms an appropriate background for the mood of darkness, but Campion does not attempt to translate his wonderful poem into musical equivalents as Dowland translated a much slighter poem on a similar subject (*In darkness let me dwell*). The music of Campion's song suggests not a season in hell but a gentle melancholy. This melancholy strain is continued in the next song, *Follow thy Saint*, the music of which contains no reference to that of *Followe thy faire sunne*, and little that is intensely memorable.

After this absorption with sorrow, the eleventh song, *Faire, if you expect admiring* (see p. 36) brings back radiance and simplicity. The harmony of the first four bars is based entirely on two chords, which enhances the striking effect of false relation in the 5th and 6th bars and of the flattened seventh for words of entreaty or sorrow; a similar effect occurs in the 9th and 10th bars. The quicker notes for the words 'bury my desires' and 'flie to her againe' suggest a release from tension.

The twelfth song, *Thou art not faire*, is in slow triple time and in a minor key–a dark sequel to the radiance of number 11; Campion was fond of this musical framework for this kind of poem (cf. *Blame not my cheeks* and *Though you are yoong*–the latter, like this, a dark sequel to a radiant song). The false relations–e.g. that in the second bar, though commonly found in

Elizabethan music, seem to illustrate well the words 'not faire' and 'not sweet'.

The thirteenth song, *See where she flies* (p. 69) is brilliantly descriptive. The varied moods and phrases of the poem are translated into rhythmic equivalents–in contrast with some other songs (e.g. *When to her lute*, number 6) in which key-changes seem to reflect the varying moods. The flight and fury are interpreted by irregular rhythms and agitated accompaniment, her spite by deliberate repeated notes; then, on the words

SEE WHERE SHE FLIES

Mil - lions of de - lights in - vent - ing;
To her beau - ties sweete con - tent - ing.

2

My fortune hangs upon her brow,
   For as she smiles or frownes on mee,
So must my blowne affections bow;
And her proude thoughts too well do find
   With what unequal tyrannie,
Her beauties doe command my mind.
      Though, when her sad planet raignes,
        Froward she bee,
     She alone can pleasure move,
      And displeasing sorrow banish.
     May I but still hold her love,
      Let all other comforts vanish.

'but when her appeased minde yeelds to delight', there is a change to triple time and gentle harmony, and a playful busy-ness of crotchets in duple time follows on the words 'all her thoughts are made of joies'. Campion's favourite flattened seventh is aptly introduced for the references to 'the winde' and 'the voice of heav'ns huge thunder'.

Blame not my cheeks, the fourteenth song, is typical but not outstanding. The melancholy tune fits the words well but does not illuminate them with any brilliant musical equivalents of poetic image or description. Robert Jones, who also set these words, pays less respect to their spirit and remains quite cheerful while 'Poore Cupid sits and blowes his nailes for cold'.

When the God of merrie love has a lively, straightforward setting which brings out the humour of the poem. The stanza of seven lines enables Campion to avoid a four-square quality that mars some of his songs.

The next three songs (16, 17 and 18) also appear, with revised versions both of words and music, in Campion's later books of airs. The first of these, *Mistris, since you so much desire*, is much inferior to the later version (IV, 22), which has greater rhythmic freedom and follows the natural accentuation of the words more closely; there is also more freedom and independence in the lute part of the later version. The next song, *Your faire lookes*, and its later version (IV, 23) have settings which are basically similar and not particularly interesting. *The man of life upright* (No. 18) appears in a completely different version in (I, 2). Neither version is very distinguished, but the first is enlivened by some syncopation; the second version is rhythmically dull and the melody moves entirely by step.

Harke, al you ladies has an attractive melody, built up from phrases of varying length. The familiar magic of the flat seventh appears again, picking out the words 'fayry queen' in each stanza:

and also 'in the darke', 'with sweet love' and 'Lillies white'; the change to triple time on 'bids you awake' is unexpected and fresh:

When thou must home, another slow song in triple time and minor key, has a gentle and unobtrusive melancholy, but conveys nothing of the beauty and magnificence, let alone the surprises and the irony, that enrich the wonderful poem.

The last song, a setting of an exercise in quantitative metrics, is a little less artificial than the poem, though even in the musical setting the wrong emphases are disturbing (e.g. the long note on 'and' in 'Both Father and Sonne'). The rhythms are loose and give the impression of prose passages or plainsong. Its failings are opposite to those found in a number of his other religious songs, which are tediously predictable and regular; here we meet surprises, but there is little or nothing that seems inevitable.

THE POEMS OF PART II

It is commonly assumed by anthologists and others that the poems in the second part of the Rosseter Book are the work of Campion, but there is no evidence to support this view. What evidence there is would lead one to think that Campion was no more responsible for the poems – for most of them, at all events – than for the music. The relevant points can be summarised as follows.

1. In his introduction Rosseter speaks of the songs in the first part as being by Campion 'to which I have added an equall number of mine owne'. From this we have no reason to think that Rosseter chose his words on any different basis than Dowland, Jones, Morley or the other song writers who, by convention, kept their poets anonymous. Indeed, if Campion had written *all* the poems of Part II, we might have expected his friend Rosseter to mention the fact, as Cooper did on the title page of *Songs of Mourning*, for which Campion wrote the words.

2. The poems of Part II are different in style and, for the most part, strikingly inferior in quality to those of Part I; indeed, while Campion's poems surpass those of the other lute-song books, the poems of Part II are well below the general level. Some of them seem like clumsy imitations of the matter and manner of Campion: e.g. number 18 ('What is a day, what is a yeere Of vaine delight and pleasure?') which is a poor shadow of Campion's 'What if a day, or a month, or a yeare'; or number 2, which calls to mind Campion's 'There is a Garden in her face':

> And would you see my Mistris face?
> It is a flowrie garden place,

> Where knots of beauties have such grace
>> That all is worke and nowhere space . . .
>
> It is the heavens bright reflexe,
>> Weake eies to dazle and to vexe,
> It is th' Idaea of her sexe,
>> Envie of whome doth world perplexe . . .

A glance at Campion's poem shows what a gulf separates the two. Each of Campion's stanzas adds a new element, and the whole piece is knit firmly together by sense and sound; in contrast, the poem in Part II is a dull catalogue of clichés, with no structural tension, with forced rhymes and with imperfect meanings.

The book is full of fustian; e.g.

> Yet still I live, and waste my wearie daies in grones,
> And with wofull tunes adorne dispayring mones.

Both logic and language often come to grief, as in these lines:

> Let lofty humors mount up on high,
>> Down againe like to the wind,
> While privat thoghts, vow'd to love,
>> More peace and plesure find.

Metre sometimes disintegrates altogether, as in the second stanza of *When Laura smiles*:

> The sprites that remaine in fleeting aire
> Affect for pastime to untwine her tressed haire,
> And the birds thinke sweete Aurora, mornings Queene
>> doth shine
> From her bright sphere, when Laura shewes her
>> lookes devine.

It is hard to conceive that Campion would create such havoc among his syllables. In the fourteenth poem we have doggerel in lame poulter's measure:

> Every day it is renu'd, and every night it bleedes,
> And with bloudy streames of sorrow drownes all our better deedes.

'Shall I come, if I swim?', the twelfth poem, has been praised by T. S. Eliot, but its rhythmic awkwardness–as of words tailored to fit a tune–links it with the other Rosseter poems rather than with those by Campion.

F

3. When Campion indents the beginnings of his lines, the grouping is by rhyme; this is not so in the poems of Part II (e.g. numbers 13, 14, 15 and 20). Another feature which does not appear in Campion's work is the poem in quatrains of short lines with a single rhyme (e.g. numbers 2 and 8), a jingling and graceless form.

4. While several of the poems of Part I were printed again, later, in modified versions, none of those in Part II was reprinted.

R. W. Berringer[1] has pointed out that the poems of Part I have some of the robust spirit of Donne and Jonson, rejoicing in physical embraces, while those in Part II are in the languishing Petrarchan tradition of hopeless adoration. He presents another piece of evidence to support the separate authorship of the poems of Parts I and II; in the first edition of Francis Davison's miscellany, *A Poetical Rapsody* (1602), a group of four poems is credited to Campion, one of them being from Part II of Rosseter's *Booke of Ayres*; the second edition of *A Poetical Rapsody*, which appeared in 1608, has the word 'Anon' under this poem, though Campion's name still appears under the other three poems in the group, suggesting that someone had pointed out an error in the first edition. A further clue is suggested in L. P. Wilkinson's evidence[2] that Campion frequently borrowed from Propertius, as shown in examples from his Books of Airs and from Rosseter's *Booke of Ayres*, Part I, but not from Part II.

Unlike the majority of the lute-song books, the second Rosseter Book contains no poem which is known to be the work of a particular author; moreover, there are certain features common to many of the poems which point to a single authorship, and it seems likely that Rosseter followed the example of Campion and wrote his own words. But two of the poems (numbers 19 and 21) are so much better than the rest and so strikingly reminiscent of Campion in style that we may suspect Rosseter had them from his friend:

> Kinde in unkindnesse, when will you relent
> And cease with faint love true love to torment?
> Still entertain'd, excluded still I stand;
> Her glove stil holde, but cannot touch the hand.

---

[1] *Thomas Campion's share in A Booke of Ayres*, PMLA, 1943, Vol. 58, p. 938.
[2] 'Propertius and Thomas Campion', *London Magazine*, 1967, Vol. 7, p. 57.

This has the intensity of experience and the crispness of epigram which characterise some of Campion's best poetry. Similar qualities emerge in the last poem of the book, which recalls and, in one line, all but quotes words of the melancholy Jaques:

> Whether men doe laugh or weepe,
> Whether they doe wake or sleepe,
> Whether they die yoong or olde,
> Whether they feele heate or colde;
> There is, underneath the sunne,
> Nothing in true earnest done.
>
> All our pride is but a jest;
> None are worst, and none are best;
> Griefe, and joy, and hope, and feare,
> Play their Pageants every where:
> Vaine opinion all doth sway,
> And the world is but a play . . .

5

RHYME AND RHYTHM

In his *Apology for Poetry* Sidney complained that the art had fallen 'from almost the highest estimation of learning to be the laughing stock of children'; of much poetry written in England he said 'it will be found that one verse did but beget another . . . which becomes a confused mass of words with a tingling sound of rhyme, barely accompanied with reason'.[1] Such laments were common in the years of critical ferment that came before the great wave of Elizabethan poetry. The Puritans had attacked poetry on moral and social grounds, and the poets and lovers of poetry, in their defence, were driven to an agonising self-appraisal. 'I scorne and spue out the rakehelly rout of our ragged Rymers',[2] wrote 'E.K.' in his dedication of Spenser's *Shepheard's Calender*; and Ascham abused 'our beggarly ryming, brought first into Italie by Gothes and Hunnes, when all good verses and all good learning too were destroyed by them'.[3]

Even in this day of metrical tolerance we must agree with some of the diatribes against verse written in the fifteenth and sixteenth centuries, including work of the leading poets. After Chaucer's technical mastery it is strange to find the groping irregularities of Lydgate and Surrey, the near-doggerel of Skelton and the metronomic banality of 'Poulter's Measure'. Verse form was varied during this transitional period, but with a variety that suggests instability rather than richness; a reaching out for solid ground which was not discovered until the language itself began to crystallise at the end of the sixteenth century.

In their search for stability and formal excellence many English writers looked back for guidance to the Greek and Latin classics, and tried to acclimatise epic hexameters and other

[1] *English Critical Essays (Sixteenth, Seventeenth and Eighteenth Centuries)* (ed. Edmund D. Jones), Oxford, 1943, pp. 2, 53.

[2] Epistle Dedicatory to *The Shepheard's Calender* in *Elizabethan Critical Essays* (ed. G. G. Smith), 1904, Vol. 1, 131.

[3] From *The Scholemaster*, in *Elizabethan Critical Essays* (ed. G. G. Smith), Vol. 1, p. 29.

unrhymed classical metres in which the length or 'quantity' rather than the stress or accent of syllables determined the rhythmic movement of the verse. Some believed that rhyme was to blame for the neglect of metre, that accentual verse was inevitably monotonous, and that quantitative verse was varied and 'decorous'. The leading theorists and experimenters were Ascham, Thomas Drant, Abraham Fraunce, William Webbe and the circle of Sidney, Spenser, Gabriel Harvey and Edward Dyer. With the exception of Drant, who regarded accent as an irrelevance, these men recognised that poetry must conform with the pattern of spoken English in which syllabic accent is of primary importance. George Puttenham recommended that accent should in English verse play the part that quantity had played in Latin, and Sidney and Spenser soon abandoned their experiments in quantity for a poetry which made full use of rhyme and accent.

As a Latin scholar Campion was not unnaturally attracted by the idea that English poetry could be trained to the civilised habits of Augustan Rome; as a sensitive poet he was appalled, as Sidney had been, by the recent chaos of English versification – even (unlike Sidney) by the Italianate sonneteering of the 1590s; lastly, as a musician (one, moreover, who set his own words) he had what might be called a vested interest in prosodic quantity. So the publication in 1602 of his *Observations in the Art of English Poesie, wherein it is demonstratively prooved . . . that the English toong will receive eight severall kinds of numbers* is not, in itself, surprising. What is hard to understand is that he put these ideas in print some years after the original Latinist craze had died down; all the more so since he had by this time achieved maturity as a poet in the rhyming idiom which he attacks in his essay. His reluctance to appear as part-author of Rosseter's Book the year before contrasts with his readiness six years earlier to print a collection of Latin poems under his own name; and from this we can, perhaps, guess that Campion, the scholar-gentleman, was embarrassed to find himself drawn into bad company by that other Campion, the song-maker.[1] The *Observations* look, at

[1] See footnote on page 47. This may have been an attempt by Campion, who had probably served under the Earl of Essex, to reinstate himself; the complimentary sapphic ode on Queen Elizabeth in the *Observations* is consistent with this idea.

first sight, like an impassioned protest of the respectable scholar; but his *alter ego* breaks in and rescues the book from dullness with a little true poetry, some good blank verse and a page of tomfoolery.

The essay is dedicated to the veteran Thomas Sackville, Lord Buckhurst, at that time Lord High Treasurer of England, but co-author forty years before of *Gorboduc*, a play which had won Sidney's approval but had now been swept away with all the other Senecan tragedies on the flood-tide of mature Elizabethan drama. In the dedication Campion praises his patron's verses ('who would not strive to imitate them?') and promises to make up later for this 'simple present' with some offering 'drawne from his more serious studies' (presumably Latin verses). There follow thirteen lines of blank verse entitled *The Writer to his Booke*; an odd, *staccato* expostulation, seemingly as far from the strict numbers which he advocates—and from *Gorboduc*—as a racy dialogue in a Ben Jonson comedy. Bullen detects in it the influence of Persius:

> Whether thus hasts my little booke so fast?
> To Paules Churchyard. What? in those cels to stand,
> With one leafe like a riders cloke put up
> To catch a termer? or lye mustie there . . . ?
> Some will redeeme me. Fewe. Yes, reade me too.
> Fewer. Nay love me. Now thou dot'st, I see . . .
> . . . Alas, poor booke, I rue
> Thy rash selfe-love; goe, spread thy pap'ry wings:
> Thy lightnes can not helpe or hurt my fame.

Obviously he did not rank the *Observations* with his important work, and may perhaps have devised it largely as a debating proposition, or legalistic argument (which later received its proper reply in Daniel's *Defence of Ryme*). From his own account it seems that he was assembling the gist of recent conversations or letters 'that they might prove the lesse troublesome in perusing'. His own subsequent writings were not in any way modified in accordance with the views he put forward so vigorously in the *Observations*.

The treatise begins by stressing that the metre of a poem depends not so much on the number of its syllables as on their value, which (as in music) is expressed by 'the length and shortnes of their sound . . . their waite and due proportion'. By introducing a neutral term, 'weight', which might refer either to length or to stress, he seems to imply some correspondence between them. And then follows an apparent irrelevance: in the setting of words to music nothing, he says, offends the ear more than placing a long syllable with a short note and a short syllable with a long note. This, however, is explained by a reference to the Renaissance mystique: 'The world is made by Simmetry and proportion, and is in that respect compared to Musick, and Musick to Poetry . . .' In other words, what applies in music should apply also in poetry. Learning, he continues, flourished among the Greeks and Romans, but became deformed and barbarised throughout the Dark Ages while it rested in the hands of ignorant monks. In those barbaric times Italians invented 'the vulgar and easie kind of Poesie . . . which we abusively call Rime'–a poor substitute for rhythm.

Campion then examines the deficiencies of rhyme. He concedes that any critic of rhymed verse will encounter glorious enemies, and experts who can 'if neede be extempore (as they say) rime a man to death'. The facility and popularity of rhyme 'creates as many Poets as a hot sommer flies'. But rhyme is a rhetorical figure and should as such be used sparingly lest it offend the ear; for comparison he cites certain ridiculous alliterative pamphlets (e.g. *Proelia porcorum*). The use of rhyme leads to a carelessness about metre; if the poet had observed quantity he could not have written such a line as

Was it my desteny, or dismall chaunce

in which the two short syllables of 'dĕstĭnў' have to fill out a whole foot. Another fault of rhyme (in sonnets, for example) is that it makes a man 'extend a short conceit beyond all bounds of arte'; as a result, the writer is often ashamed of what he has written. What divine or politician would quote a rhyme? Contrast the 'noble Grecians and Romaines', whose philosophers often quoted poetry, and whose scriptures were in verse. No doubt the famous Italian, French and Spanish poets who used rhyme would, if given the chance, prefer to see their books translated into the 'auncient numbers' of Greece and Rome. 'What honour were it then for our English language to be the first that after so many yeares of barbarisme could second the perfection of the industrious Greekes and Romaines?'

Campion then proceeds to show how, in his opinion, this might be achieved. Of the three principal feet used in Greek and Latin poetry, the dactylic is clearly unsuited for use in English with its numerous monosyllables and heavy polysyllabic words; but the other two (the iambic and the trochaic) are well suited and often used unconsciously and 'without the guidance of arte' by English writers. In stressing the ineptness of English dactylic verse, he points out how often those who have attempted it used such borrowed words as 'Amyntas', 'Avernus', 'Olympus' and so on.

Campion then brings his musical ear to aid his judgment on a question of verse prosody:

> I have observed, and so may any one that is either practis'd in singing, or hath a naturall eare able to time a song, that the Latine verses of sixe feete, as the *Heroick* and *Iambick*, or of five feete, as the *Trochaick*, are in nature all of the same length of sound with our English verses of five feete; for either of them being tim'd with the hand . . . they fill up the quantity (as it were) of five sem'briefs.

This, he adds, can be explained by the heaviness of our syllables, and the number of rests or breathing pauses that have to be allowed in the middle of lines and between lines.

Saying no more about accent and quantity, he goes on to describe and illustrate pure and 'licentiate' iambics in English, the latter allowing use of a spondee, a dactyl, a tribrach or even an anapaest in place of an iambus for the first, second and fourth feet; even the third and fifth feet, which are generally iambic, may be filled by a tribrach:

> Mēn thāt | dŏ fāll | tŏ mĭsĕ|rў, quīck|lў fāll.
> Rĕnōwn'd | ĭn ēv'|rў ārt | thēre līves | nŏt ănў.

From these specimens (in which we have indicated quantities not marked in the original) it is clear that Campion does not equate stress with length of syllable; the first syllable of 'misery', for example, he counts as short, though it takes a natural stress, as in this line from *King Lear*:

> We scarcely think our miseries our foes.

In most feet of the illustrative verse, however, Campion makes a long syllable coincide with a stress, and there is no problem of scansion. Considered as accentual verse the lines are natural and varied–which, with all the liberty Campion allows himself, is not unexpected. Few readers are likely to diagnose the following lines of blank verse as an experiment in quantity:

> Goe, numbers, boldly passe, stay not for ayde
> Of shifting rime, that easie flatterer,
> Whose witchcraft can the ruder eares beguile.
> Let your smoothe feete, enur'd to purer arte,
> True measures tread. What if your pace be slow
> And hops not like the Grecian elegies?
> It is yet gracefull, and well fits the state
> Of words ill-breathed and not shap't to runne.
>
> Goe then, but slowly, till your steps be firme;
> Tell them that pitty or perversely skorne
> Poore English Poesie as the slave to rime,
>   You are those loftie numbers that revive
> Triumphes of Princes and sterne tragedies . . .

Repeatedly Campion tells the poet to follow the judgment of his ear, and his advice often seems to us reasonable; as when, for example, he says that one should place a spondee, a dactyl or a tribrach after an opening trochee, 'for an Iambick beginning with a single short sillable, and the other ending before with the like, would too much drinke up the verse if they came immediately together'. His illustrations of these precepts, however, appear to us grotesque, and from Daniel's remarks we may take it that such scansion as the following must have appeared strange to his contemporaries too:

> Nōblĕ, | īngĕnĭ|ŏus, ānd | dīscrēet|lў wīse.

Pronounced and accented as modern English this line is euphonious, and answers Campion's auditory criterion:

> Nóble, ingénious ànd discréetly wíse.

But what reason can there be for regarding the first three syllables of 'ingenious' as a dactyl? The natural stress on the second syllable gives it greater length or 'weight' than the third syllable carries, and its quasi-dactylic nature is only detectable to the eye. This seems to make nonsense of Campion's advice to the writer, that he should make his iambic verse a little more licentiate 'that it might thereby imitate our common talk'.

After considering the iambic pentameter, Campion goes on to discuss the iambic dimeter or 'English march', which he describes as 'our most naturall and auncient English verse'. He illustrates the form with a tragic chorus, a lyric and an epigram:

> Kind in every kinde
> This, deare Ned, resolve.
> Never of thy prayse
> Be too prodigall;
> He that prayseth all
> Can praise truly none.

Next comes a chapter on 'trochaic verse'–pentameters in which the first foot is a spondee, a trochee or an iambus, and the remaining feet are all trochees. This form he finds particularly well suited for epigrams (e.g. 'Barnzy stiffly vows that hees no Cuckold;' see page 21). He excuses himself for alluding to people by their real names in the illustrations, pointing out that he does so to make the style appear the more English, 'without offence to any person'.

The next chapter is about 'English Elegeick verse', by which Campion means couplets consisting of a 'licentiate' iambic pentameter followed by a line consisting of two dimeters:

> Constant to none, but ever false to me,
>   Traiter still to love through thy faint desires,
> Not hope of pittie now nor vaine redresse
>   Turns my griefs to teares and renu'd laments.
> Too well thy empty vowes and hollow thoughts
>   Witnes both thy wrongs and remorseles hart . . .

Campion offers this form as the nearest that English syllables can be made to approach the quality of Greek and Latin elegiac couplets, but the experiment can hardly be called a success. In contrast with the balance of the classical couplet, the lines of the 'English elegiac' couplet clash and do not seem to belong to each other; the reader must readjust his ear at the end of each line. It is odd, too, that Campion, having found the English iambic pentameter equal in length to the classical hexameter, should not find the double dimeter, with its six stresses, overweight as a partner for the iambic line.

The eighth chapter, 'Of Ditties and Odes', is concerned with lyrical poems, by which Campion means poems suitable for singing to the accompaniment of an instrument. As almost all of his own poetry is of this type, we might expect to find here something of special interest and perhaps a key to his ideas and practices on the integration of words with music. All that we are given, in fact, are three specimen poems illustrating different verse forms. There is a dull sapphic ode on a shower which cheated the people of their promised glimpse of the Queen:

> But whence showres so fast this angry tempest,
> Clowding dimme the place? Behold, Eliza
> This day shines not here; this heard, the launces
>   And thick heads do vanish.

The next verse form is illustrated by the well-known anthology piece, *Rose cheekt Lawra*; after which comes another pleasing poem in a similar form:

>   Just beguiler,
>   Kindest love, yet only chastest,
>   Royall in thy smooth denyals,
>   Frowning or demurely smiling,
>   Still my pure delight . . .

The ninth and last form is an anacreontic ode consisting of trochaic dimeters; a form 'too licentiate for a higher place, and in respect of the rest imperfect'; yet very suitable for madrigals 'or any other lofty or tragicall matter', as in the example:

>   Follow, followe,
>   Though with mischiefe
>   Arm'd like whirlewind
>   Now she flyes thee;
>   Time can conquer
>   Loves unkindnes;
>   Love can alter
>   Times disgraces;
>   Till death faint not
>   Then but followe . . .

Offering these metres which 'were never before by any man attempted', Campion recommended others to imitate and amplify the medium. Some, he admits, may object to the cadence of these verses through being 'accustomed to the fatnes of rime'; but if anyone examines them with a judicious ear he will realise that the lines close naturally, and that rhyme would be not only superfluous but absurd. This conclusion, however, cannot be accepted, for in almost all of the examples the metrical effect is similar to the effects which he produced in his rhymed verse of the song books. The accents are well spaced and fall naturally; it is hard to believe that in writing them Campion used a technique different from that which he used in his other verse.

The treatise ends with a chapter on the quantitative value of English syllables. It refers to the Latin rule of 'position', by which any vowel becomes long if it is followed by two or more consonants. This and other classical rules are tacitly accepted (though with much licence) as applicable in English; e.g. that a diphthong is long; that the opening syllable 're' is always short (unless lengthened by position); that the opening syllable 'de' in trisyllabic words is long; that a vowel followed by another vowel is always short (e.g. flȳing) 'unless the accent alter it [as] in dĕnȳing'. In the last example accent is seen to have the predominant influence over quantity. Indeed, from one passage it must be concluded that Campion does not make any clear and consistent distinction between accent and length of syllable:

> Neither can I remember any impediment except position that can alter the *accent* [our italics] of any sillable in our English verse. For though we accent the second of 'Trumpington' short, yet is it naturally long, and so of necessity must be held of every composer. Wherefore the first rule that is to be observed is the nature of the accent, which we must ever follow.

The second syllable of 'Trumpington' may be considered long by 'position', and it is unaccented; but to speak of it as being 'accented short' is to confuse the nomenclature of stress and quantity. Another oddity is the suggestion that words like 'appear' and 'oppose' with double consonants should keep their first syllables short by being read as though they were spelt 'apear' and 'opose'; this conversion (in modern English, at least) would actually have the opposite effect of lengthening the first syllable by placing an accent upon it.

It is hard to believe that Campion was deeply concerned about quantity, and in spite of the dogmas he invokes, the examples he offers are refreshingly free from 'dranting' distortion. The one striking exception appears not in the *Observations* but in the earlier Rosseter Book, where it is described by Campion as the only song in that book written after the manner of Greek and Latin poets who tied themselves 'strictly to number and value of their sillables'. 'Come let us sound with melody the praises' would pass for a line of English verse, but who would guess that it is a sapphic with the following scansion:

'Cōme lĕt ūs sōund wīth mĕlŏdȳ thĕ praīses . . .'

or that the marks over the syllables in the following lines have anything to do with metre:

'Hīs dĕvīne pŏwĕr ānd glŏrĭe, thēnce hĕ thūnders,
One ĭn āll, ānd āll stĭll ĭn ōne ăbīding,
    Bōth Făthĕr ānd Sŏnne'?

Campion, of course, does not insert these marks; what he does, instead, is to fit the words to a tune which is in sapphic metre. It has been cited as an example of *musique mesurée*; but while the writers of the Pléiade insisted that music should follow the long and short syllables of the verse, Campion made his verses follow the long and short syllables of a tune in sapphic metre, provided the Latin rules of prosody were observed by the verses.

There is no *a priori* argument against the distortion of natural speech-values in song—or even in a kind of *Sprechgesang*; to appreciate 'Come, let us sound with melody' as an ode in sapphic metre, some distortion of this sort is inevitable. But even if a volatile impulse had led Campion to recommend such exercises in Rosseter's Book, the precept and example of the *Observations* clearly reveal his second thoughts on the subject, as in the following passage: 'above all the accent of our words is diligently to be observ'd, for chiefly by the accent in any language the true value of the sillables is to be measured.'

What, then, was Campion's purpose in putting forward the case for quantity in English verse? From his confused argument it might seem that he was deceiving himself more than his readers, but the confusion has obscured what may be the real interest of his thoughts on this subject. Under the rhetoric we can distinguish a passion for balance, a determination that each line of verse shall be filled with the correct proportion of weight, stress, pitch and silence. R. W. Short[1] has pointed out that Campion was trying to regularise the use of quantities by rules corresponding in importance to the accepted rules of accentuation and thus to bring back a *conscious* control over the time element in verse. He regards the poetry of the song books as a better illustration of Campion's use of these ideas than the specimens in the *Observations*. From the subsequent history of English poetry we can see how unnecessary such rules have been and how the language dictates its own much subtler metrical variety and proportion, as, for example, in this:

> The sedge is withered from the lake
> And no birds sing.

But Campion, with his background of 'ragged rymers'—and a legal training—must have considered the book of rules a reasonable provision against the familiar excesses and deficiencies.

Apart from its disciplinary function, however, the control of quantity must have appealed to Campion—as it did to Robert Bridges three hundred years later—by enriching the verse medium with a second dimension. In the English language accent and quantity are partially independent variables, and simultaneous attention to both is analogous with hearing two lines of music in polyphony. Speaking of the second line of *Paradise Lost*, Bridges points out that the word 'forbidden' is stressed on its shortest syllable, the second, and he complains that English writers on metre commonly confuse accent with quantity.[2] The English word 'hexameter' is another illustration of the separation of accent and quantity, for the stress is commonly placed on the second syllable, though it is shorter than the first. But in English, the disposition of long and short syllables is less clearly defined than it appears to be in Latin, and the use of quantity in verse must, for that reason, always seem experimental rather than inevitable.

---

[1] R. W. Short, 1944, PMLA, LIX, 1003.
[2] *Milton's Prosody*, Oxford, 1921, pp. 2–3.

The spearhead of Daniel's reply[1] was directed against the renunciation of rhyme. With a self-assurance matching that of Campion he claimed that he had in his essay 'demonstratively proved that Ryme is the fittest harmonie of wordes that comportes with our language'. He presents his case with subtlety and scores many debating points over his illustrious but muddled opponent. Beginning with a compliment to the king, the Countess of Pembroke and to all the other 'worthie lovers and learned professors of ryme', he sympathises with them in their dismay at being charged with a 'grosse, vulgare and barbarous' practice 'which if it be so, we have lost much labour to no purpose'. He blames Campion, 'whose commendable Rymes . . . have given heretofore to the world the best notice of his worth' for a lack of charity; if he had proved his ability without disparaging his fellows, they would gladly have stood quietly by him.

In his defence of rhyme Daniel claims that it adds more grace and gives more delight 'than ever bare numbers, howsoever they can be forced to runne in our slow language, can possibly yeeld'. He asserts, moreover, that rhyme gives a finer harmony than any verse form which antiquity has shown us, and the fact that it is universally accepted not only in England but by other nations argues that it cannot be merely dismissed as 'an ill custome'. Against Campion's protest that rhyme is a rhetorical figure and should be sparingly used, Daniel says 'tyrannicall Rules of idle Rhetorique' must bow to custom; against Campion's argument that a poet is apt to stretch his matter to fit the rhyme, Daniel argues that rhyme, on the contrary, prevents the matter from 'running wildely on like a tedious fancie without a close'. The fact that some poets rhyme badly does not mean that rhyme itself is bad; the 'eminent spirit' is not hampered but carried to higher flights by the use of rhyme.

Then, with more questionable daring, Daniel carries the attack against the citadel itself, complaining of the excessive poetic licence and the torturing of sentences in Greek and Latin poetry; we admire the classics for their matter, and in spite of their medium. Why, then, should we ape Greece or Italy? Nature is a better model, and so, for that matter, are the great men who adorned Italy and other European countries at a time when, in

[1] *A Defence of Ryme* (?1603), in *Elizabethan Critical Essays* (ed. G. G. Smith), 1904, Vol. II, p. 356.

Campion's mistaken view, learning was still in the hands of illiterate monks.

The attack is now directed against Campion: 'Our adversary' has given us no masterpiece . . . 'to deprave the present forme of writing and to bring us nothing but a few loose and uncharitable epigrammes . . . giveth us cause to suspect the performance.' First, he says, we are told to imitate the Greeks and Romans, and then shown how to disobey their rules. Campion's forms themselves turn out to be nothing more than traditional English metres with new names attached; though sometimes we are asked to mispronounce our language (e.g. in lengthening the last syllable of 'desolate' and 'funeral').

In conclusion he concedes two points to Campion: first, that there is much poor rhymed verse being written; and second, that blank verse is most suitable for tragedy. And then, a sly dig at Campion's portentousness:

> the greatest hinderer to our proceedings is this Selfe-love, whereunto we Versifiers are ever noted to be specially subject . . . for there is not the simplest writer that will ever tell himselfe that he doth ill . . . but perswades him that his lines cannot but please others which so much delight himselfe . . . and the more to shew that he is so, we shall see him evermore in all places and to all persons repeating his owne compositions. . . .

Daniel's essay did more than puncture the conceit and the weak logic of Campion's thesis; in Vivian's words it 'finally demolished the craze against rhyming of which Campion's was the final statement'. This is, perhaps, putting it too strongly; Milton introduced the blank verse of *Paradise Lost* with an assertion that rhyme was 'no necessary adjunct or true ornament of poem or good verse, in longer works especially, being the invention of a barbarous age, to set off wretched matter and lame metre', and Collins, in his famous ode *To Evening*, showed how a perfect English lyric could be written without rhyme. But the desire to rhyme is inescapable—even today. Ben Jonson is said to have refuted both Campion and Daniel, but the work in which he expressed these views is lost. Campion's unconditional surrender is surmised from the consistent use of rhyme in all his later poetry.

Apart from giving us a glimpse of Campion's ideas on the grammar of verse, the *Observations* reveal something, obliquely, of Campion's restless state of mind, and of a preoccupation with matters that were to engage his time more fully during the next three years. This emerges in some of the epigrams; in the one on Hurst, the banker, for example, whose bones were 'all growne so pockie and so rotten'; and in this:

> Lockly spits apace, the rhewme he cals it,
> But no drop (though often urgd) he straineth
> From his thirstie jawes, yet all the morning
> And all day he spits, in ev'ry corner;
> At his meales he spits, at every meeting . . .
> Yet no cost he spares; he sees the Doctors,
> Keeps a strickt diet, precisely useth
> Drinks and bathes drying, yet all prevailes not,
> 'Tis not *China* (*Lockly*), *Salsa Guacum*,
> Nor dry *Sassafras* can help, or ease thee;
> Tis no humor hurts, it is thy humor.

Three years after the publication of this, Campion took his doctorate of medicine at Caen; but from the remarks about Lockly we may conjecture that his medical studies had already begun in 1602.

G

6

THE MASQUES

THE Renaissance hunger for allegory, for enjoyment and for display is richly expressed in the Tudor and early Stuart court masques. One might have expected an ideal synthesis of art from this form on which such varied talent and so much enthusiasm were lavished; yet of all the artistic products of that age the masque is the most dated. Perhaps, as Francis Bacon hinted,[1] we should not take these 'toys' too seriously; but the rulers and the nobility took them seriously enough, as we can judge from the fabulous sums they were prepared to spend upon such ephemeral entertainment.[2]

Their interest for us is largely historical, for the Masque is the link between a folk tradition of seasonal dances and pageants and the living arts of opera and ballet. Enid Welsford has described how the Masque from its origins 'consisted in the arrival of certain persons vizored and disguised to dance a dance or present an offering'.[3] These ingredients are also found in certain primitive and almost world-wide rituals associated with agricultural festivals. In mediaeval England processions of people disguised with beasts' heads or discoloured faces entered their neighbours' houses at Christmas and Shrovetide to dance or play at dice. These 'mummeries' and other rituals, some of them of pre-Christian origin, were enriched in the fifteenth century by features drawn from the religious drama. Poets began to write verses for them, and the ritual became an art rich in symbol and allegory, known as the *disguising*. A further development came in 1513 when the young Henry VIII, copying the Italian *mascheria*, made his performers choose ladies in the audience for dancing partners and entertain them with 'gallant' conversation. This performance, which was described as a *maske*, became accepted

---

[1] Essays: *Of Masques and Triumphs.*

[2] *English Masques* (ed. H. A. Evans), Blackie, London, 1897.

[3] *The Court Masque: A Study in the Relationship between Poetry and the Revels*, Cambridge, 1927, p. 3.

in Tudor England as the pattern for entertainment of royal visitors on festival days or during their 'progresses' through the country, and for the celebration of weddings of the nobility. Famous poets, composers and architects were engaged for the preparation of these maskes (or masques, as they were later spelt).

Similar entertainments were popular at the courts of continental Europe. In Italy, the development of monodic vocal music and the recitative at the end of the sixteenth century provided a technique by which the Court masque or masquerade could be re-created as the new and vital art of opera. In France, the classical ballet was created as the result of experiments in the fusion of Italian masquerade with the French spectacular tournament. Both styles drew inspiration from classical Greek drama.

Although the English masque was described by French visitors as 'ballet',[1] its development was in various ways different from that which took place in France and in Italy. Each of its ingredients—poetry, music, dialogue, dancing and *décor*—increased in complexity, the emphasis depending to a great extent on the inclinations of the artist or artists who devised the masque. Its greatest and most prolific exponent, Ben Jonson, tried to achieve a classic balance between the ingredients; being a poet and a dramatist of genius, he enriched his masques with splendid verse and dialogue. His great collaborator, Inigo Jones, stressed the spectacular elements and stagecraft. The popular demand was for more spectacle, more clowning, more song and dance; so the masque became hypertrophied into crudely gorgeous spectacle and degraded to pantomime before the Commonwealth swept it away.[2] Though music was an important component of English masques (even recitative was used for the dialogue in Jonson's *Vision of Delight* and *Lovers made Men*)[3], operatic form did not emerge from the masque in England. Its outstanding feature was poetry, and its significant transformation was into the masque elements of Shakespeare's plays and the poetic masques of Milton. It has been suggested that music drama in England

---

[1] Ibid., p. 164.
[2] Ibid., p. 243.
[3] H. A. Evans, *English Masques*, op. cit., p. 124; see also A. J. Sabol, *Songs and Dances*, Providence, 1959.

was 'nipped in the bud by poetry';[1] but when we see what liberties the Restoration took with Shakespeare it seems unlikely that the excellence of Shakespeare's poetry was to blame for the absence of indigenous opera. In English masques, and especially in those of Campion, music was a successful vehicle for song and dance rather than for the expression of dramatic emotion.

Campion was almost perfectly fitted by talent and temperament for the composition of masques. It is true that his masques show little evidence of dramatic ability, but drama was a relatively unimportant aspect of the masque. Campion's ability to produce both music and poetry in a unified design made up for deficiencies in the dialogue. As a student at Gray's Inn he had collaborated with Francis Davison in the preparation of the *Masque of Proteus* (1594), which Enid Welsford has described as a turning-point in the history of the masque, and 'the first piece that we know of which gives the norm of the masque as composed by Ben Jonson and his fellow poets'.[2] The only part of this masque which is generally accepted to be the work of Campion is the opening song, *Of Neptunes Empyre let us sing*; it was included over the name 'H. Campion' in Francis Davison's *Poetical Rapsody* (1602), and appeared in a slightly different version in Nichols' *Progresses of Queen Elizabeth*. An anthologists' favourite, this poem has the air of words written for music and several features that remind one of Campion's later song lyrics, a rhythmic felicity, a generalised visual imagery, and a lover's particularity about the sounds of music:

> The Sea-Nymphes chaunt their Accents shrill,
> And the Syrens taught to kill
>   With their sweet voyce;
> Make ev'ry ecchoing Rocke reply,
> Unto their gentle murmuring noyse,
> The prayse of *Neptunes* Empery.

The preoccupation with music in the rest of the masque and the symbolic figure of Proteus as its principal character are also, perhaps, suggestive of Campion.

Campion's four published masques were produced between 1607 and 1614, at a time when the form had evolved to its full

---

[1] Eric Blom, 'A Substitute for Opera', *The Observer*, London, 16th February 1958.   [2] Welsford, op. cit., p. 163.

splendour and before the beginning of its artistic decline. Its structure at this time followed certain rules which, though elaborate, allowed the poet considerable freedom to express his fancies. The nucleus of the masque was a series of stately figure dances by members of the royal or noble household, who were called 'masquers'; they were gorgeously dressed and did not sing or speak. After the figure dances there usually came livelier dances called 'revels', for which the masquers chose partners of the opposite sex from the audience. During the first part of the performance the masquers were hidden from view, while the business of the masque was introduced by speeches or dialogue; this, from the time of Jonson's *Masque* at the Marriage of Viscount Haddington (1608), was amplified into the form of 'antimasque', in which grotesque or comic or satirical song, dialogue and dance were presented to heighten by contrast the majesty and beauty of the masquers who were then revealed in their glory. To make this moment of revelation as effective as possible, elaborate scenery, lighting and stage devices were introduced. The masquers issued from or were discovered in magnificent settings. Between the dances there were songs in praise of the masquers, calling them to rest, or encouraging them to continue, or announcing the approach of dawn and the end of the revels. The antimasque was performed by professional actors and the music by court musicians and choirboys of the Chapel Royal or St. Paul's.

The first and most elaborate of Campion's masques was presented before the King at Whitehall on Twelfth Night, 1607, to celebrate the marriage of Lord Hayes, a Scottish gentleman and a great favourite of the King, to Honora, daughter of Lord Denny. A description of the masque was published in 1607, with several dedicatory poems. The first was to King James, and in it Campion seized the occasion of a marriage between a Scot and an Englishwoman to comment on the 'high and everliving Union tweene Scots and English', and the increase of strength that would come from this marriage of kingdoms; in an epigram he hails King James as King Arthur come to life again in fulfilment of Merlin's prophecy. There follow Latin elegiacs for the king, a tribute to the chief masquer, Lord Walden, with a plea for his patronage and a conventional address to the bridegroom, with more elegiacs.

The setting of the masque is then described. In the great hall there were two stages, a lower one for the dances, and one three feet higher which was covered with a double veil painted to look as though clouds hung before it. Flanking the lower stage were three groups of musicians—ten instrumentalists on one side (bass and mean lutes, a bandora, a double sackbut, a harpsichord and two treble violins) and twelve on the other (nine violins and three lutes), with a third group of six 'chappell voyces' and six cornets which were 'in a place raised higher in respect of the pearcing sound of those Instruments'. The higher stage behind the curtains represented a green valley with trees and in the middle were 'nine golden trees of fifteene foote high, with armes and braunches very glorious to behold'. There was a broad path from this grove down to the dancing place, a path on the right to the bower of Flora, and a path on the left to the house of Night, each of which was on a hill. There was a third hill in the middle on which stood the Tree of Diana. On another hill were those who played on 'hoboyes' at the King's entrance into the hall. The bower of Flora was spacious, and full of flowers and lights. The house of Night was stately, with black pillars starred with gold; inside it were clouds and stars, and 'artificial' bats and owls were continually moving about . . . 'with many other inventions, the which for brevitie sake I passe by with silence'.

The nine masquers, representing the Knights of Apollo, are then named in order of importance—the number nine being the best of numbers, for 'in numbring after the ninth we begin again, the tenth beeing as it were the Diappason in Arithmetick'. There were four speakers: Flora, with a flowery veil and crown; Zephyrus with a mantle of white silk propped with wire and waving behind him as he moved; Night, with a black starred robe, a black face and a crown of stars; and Hesperus, in deep crimson mixed with sky colour.

The performance is now described. At the King's entrance, the hoboyes played till he and his train were seated, and then while the consort of ten instruments played an air, one of the curtains was drawn back, revealing Flora and Zephyrus attended by six silvans, four of them carrying lutes. As they gathered flowers, Zephyrus[1] and the two silvans without lutes sang and the others accompanied the song on their instruments:

[1] It was unusual for speaking characters, such as Zephyrus, to sing.

Now hath Flora rob'd her bowers
To befrend this place with flowers:
   Strowe aboute, strowe aboute . . .
   Earth hath no Princelier flowers
Then Roses white, and Roses red,
But they must still be mingled:
And as a Rose new pluckt from Venus thorne,
So doth a Bride her Bride-groomes bed adorne . . .

After the song Flora presented flowers and (in rhymed couplets) good wishes, which Zephyrus, the friend of love, echoed with prophecies of faithfulness and fruitfulness. Then came a song in dialogue, a sort of mock debate in which the cause of marriage is made to triumph over that of single life, ending with a chorus of 'Hymen, Io Hymen'.

And then, the dramatic moment: the second veil or curtain was suddenly drawn back, revealing the grove and the golden trees, the hill of Diana and the house of Night, who appeared with her nine attendant Hours, each carrying a lighted black torch. In resounding verse Night rebuked Flora for heaping insult on injury against Diana (or Cynthia), the goddess of virginity. Flora pleads, Zephyrus argues:

> Nature ordaind not Men to live alone,
> Where there are two a Woman should be one.

But in vain; for Diana has already shown her wrath against nine of Apollo's knights, turning them into trees because they attempted to seduce her nymphs; there they must stay (golden out of respect to Apollo) until Diana herself releases them.

Now Hesperus, the evening star and symbol of the approaching marriage night, descended with a message of peace: Diana has been pacified by Apollo, and is now content that her nymph should be made a bride–since the match has been graced by our British Apollo (King James); moreover, she sends a gem in token of her wish that the nine knights of Apollo should be restored to their proper shape. At once Night began to shake off her melancholy ('Who shold grace mirth and revels but the night?'). Four silvans played on their lutes, and the golden trees began to dance to a choral song:

Move now with measured sound,
You charmed grove of gould,
Trace forth the sacred ground
That shall your formes unfold.

A modern audience would smile at such nursery stuff, especially
when the chorus sings

Much joy must needs the place betide where trees for
gladnes move;

but perhaps the splendours of the music and the spectacle or
even the convention of pageantry held the Jacobean company
spellbound. (In *Macbeth* other factors—the tension of the drama
and the imminence of doom—forbid laughter when Birnam
Wood begins to move towards Dunsinane.) The trees, in groups
of three, were made to sink a yard and were left in three parts,
the masquers appearing out of their tops (these changes effected
by an 'ingin' under the stage); after which the trees were taken
away—less adroitly than was planned, 'through the simplicity,
negligence or conspiracy of the painter' (whose name does not
appear).

By stages the knights were restored to human shape, and
elaborate transformation music was played and sung. Solemnly
they descended in green robes to the dancing place, and the
chorus sang; then music was played for their dances by the
consort of twelve instruments, echoed by the cornets and the
consort of ten, playing sometimes separately and sometimes
together. Night applauded their performance, and invited them
to pay their respects to Diana, who had smiled so kindly upon
them; whereupon she led them in procession around the tree of
Diana, while the chapel choir sang a six-part motet in honour of
chastity. The knights plucked off their green robes and laid them
as offerings at the foot of Diana's tree; and then, resplendent in
carnation satin with silver lace, each preceded by a torchbearing
Hour, they moved towards the bower of Flora. This was followed
by a lively figure-dance, after which the masquers danced with
ladies in the audience. Hesperus then spoke his farewell speech,
and was sent off with a dialogue for four voices; then Night and
Flora withdrew their train, allowing the revels to break out once
more with lighter dances—corantos, levaltas and galliards, till

Night, speaking from the grove, called the revellers to their last dance:

> 'Hymen long since the Bridal bed hath drest,
> And longs to bring the turtles to their nest.
> Then with one quick dence sound up your delight,
> And with one song weele bid you all god-Night.'

The closing choral song of Silvans and Hours is light and iridescent:

> *Silvan*: Tell me, gentle howre of night,
>   Wherein dost thou most delight?
> *Houre*:   Not in sleepe.
> *Silvan*:   Wherein then?
> *Houre*: In the frolicke vew of men.
> *Silvan*: Lovest thou musicke?
> *Houre*:   O 'tis sweet.
> *Silvan*: Whats dauncing?
> *Houre*:   Ev'n the mirth of feete.
> *Silvan*: Joy you in Fayries and in elves?
> *Houre*: We are of that sort our selves . . .

After the song, the masquers removed their vizards and helmets, made a low bow to the King and attended him to the banqueting place.

In 1613 Campion published a volume containing descriptions of two masques. The first was an entertainment given by Lord Knowles (or Knollys) at Cawsome House, near Reading, to Queen Anne in her progress towards Bath. The word *Entertainment* was used in a special sense for such occasions as this, the nucleus of the form being a speech of welcome; but in Lord Knowles' entertainment, masque dances and revels were also included.

As the Queen and her train approached Cawsome House, across fields, a figure dressed in skins and leaves described as a 'Cynick' appeared out of a bower and told them not to trespass on this place of silence where he enjoys a kingdom without people, living happily on herbs and water. A courtly traveller on horseback rebuked the cynic for his presumption, dismounted, and in a short bout of pseudo-Socratic dialogue paralysed his defence:

Cynick: I am conquered by reason, and humbly aske pardon for my error; henceforth my heart shall honour greatnesse, and love so-cietie . . .

Thereupon Cynic and Traveller mounted on horseback and hastened to the Park Gate, where they were formally received by the Keepers. While the Queen proceeded, cornets played. A Keeper then made a short speech of welcome, after which the two Keepers, two Robin Hood men and the Cynic performed a part-song for trebles, counter-tenors and bass, dancing a silvan dance at the same time, while the Traveller, who can't sing, 'gapes in silence and expresseth his humour in Antike gestures'. The progress continued. The Queen stepped from her carriage and walked on carpet across the garden, where she was enter-tained with 'fragrant phrases' by a Gardener and his man and boy who carry silver spades and rakes; 'for Woods are more full of weeds then wits, but gardens are weeded, and Gardners witty, as may appear by me. I have flowers for all fancies. Tyme for truth, Rosemary for remembrance, Roses for love . . . and thousands more, which all harmoniously rejoyce at your pre-sence.' Then they sang a song for treble and bass, accompanied by instruments. The Queen climbed the steps to the upper garden, where she was greeted by song from an excellent counter-tenor accompanied by two 'unusuall instruments', both hidden.

The Queen supped privately, attended by the King's violins. After supper the entertainment was resumed in the hall. Sud-denly the Traveller, the Cynic, the Gardener and their crew entered. The Traveller declared himself an academic and a clown; the Gardener recalled how Venus put a silver spade and rake into his hand when he was an infant, transforming him at once to his present shape; which story the Traveller caps with a compliment to the royal visitor, saying that he has now seen a deity as far beyond Venus as the beauty of light is beyond darkness.

This is the signal for the transition from antimasque to masque proper. After a song, the clowns vanished. Then Silvanus, god of the woods, appeared and addressed the Queen in verse (the first verse speech of the entertainment). Eight masquers entered with pageantry and music, and the set dances were followed by revels in which the Queen took part. On the day of her departure the Gardener made a farewell speech, which was followed by more songs and an exchange of presents.

There was hardly a trace of dramatic interest but an abundance of music and some rather irrelevant buffoonery in *Lord Knowles' Entertainment*. The masque which was published with it (known as *The Lords' Masque*) is different in spirit and in texture. Like the *Masque in honour of Lord Hayes*, this one was produced for a wedding (of the Count Palatine to the Princess Elizabeth). In the Lords' Masque there is an antimasque in rhymed couplets, with grotesque elements, and the germ of dramatic movement at the start which is, of course, halted to make way for singing, dancing and flattery. The scene was prepared by Inigo Jones (whose ingenuity was praised in the text, though his name does not appear on the title-page); it has two levels, the lower of which is first revealed as a wood, with a cave on one side. Orpheus, the patron of music, summons Mania, the goddess of madness, who emerges from the cave; he rebukes her for keeping Entheus (Poetic Fury) imprisoned with other kinds of madmen, and charges her in the name of Jove to release him. Mania retorts

> How can I? Franticks with him many more
> In one cave are lockt up; ope once the dore,
> All will flie out . . .

Orpheus reassures her, saying that music can be provided which will make all the lunatics except Entheus return to their cave. Mania obeys, and the 'franticks' enter–the lover, the self-lover, the melancholic, the 'Schoole-man over-come with phantasie, the over-watched Usurer, with others that made an absolute medly of madnesse'. They dance to music at first fantastic, then solemn. Entheus is freed–in order that he might join with Orpheus and, at Jove's command, 'create inventions rare, this night to celebrate'.

After the antimasque, the upper half of the scene was un-covered, revealing a sky with clouds of several colours and 'eight Starres of extraordinarie bignesse, which so were placed, as that they seemed to be fixed betweene the Firmament and the Earth'. In the midst stood Prometheus, who joined with Orpheus and Entheus in their task of solemnising the nuptials. As the choir sang, the stars 'mooved in an exceeding strange and delightfull manner', and were then suddenly transformed into eight gor-geously dressed masquers. After a preluding dance by pages 'like

fierie spirits, all their attires being alike composed of flames',
Prometheus led the masquers on a bright cloud down to earth,
where four ladies, newly transformed from statues, awaited
them. The masquers courted them (two to one), but Jove fore-
stalled trouble by transforming four other female statues to
adjust the numbers. Choral songs accompanied their dance. The
revels followed. Later a Sibyl prophesied in Latin, an obelisk
was erected to immortalise the nuptial pair, and the pomp and
absurdity vanished in a gale of lyrical exuberance.

Campion's fourth and last masque was performed in December 1613 at the marriage of the notorious Robert Car, Earl of
Somerset, to Frances Howard. In the preface to the description
of this masque Campion prepares us for enchantments and trans-
formations. The workmanship, he tells us, was by an Italian
architect, Constantine (de Servi); though not up to expectation,
it was splendid–a triumphal arch, behind which were a 'skye of
clowdes', a high promontory on either side, the sea in perspective
with ships, some cunningly painted, some artificially sailing; in
the foreground was a garden with seats for the masquers, and a
staircase like a scallop shell.

After the King, the Queen and Prince Charles had taken their
places, four Squires entered. Each in turn addressed the throne
in rhymed couplets, telling how the knights whom they serve
(three from each corner of the earth) were attacked, while sailing
for Britain to attend this wedding, by four fiends, Error, Rumour,
Curiosity and Credulity. Tempests raged, separating the ships;
serpents appeared on board; lightning snatched the knights, six
of whom were seen by the squires to be transformed into pillars
of gold 'faire to our eyes, but wofull to beholde'.

The fiends then appeared and danced–Error like a snake,
with snakes in place of hair; Rumour in a coat full of winged
tongues; Curiosity, with eyes all over her coat and cap, and
Credulity in a similar dress adorned with ears. The four Winds
rushed in; after them, in confusion, came the four Elements, and
then the four parts of the Earth–Europe in the habit of an
empress, Asia in a Persian lady's dress, Africa like a Queen of
the Moors, and America in a skin coat with coloured feathers in
her hair. They danced together in confusion, and scattered. Now
came the Three Fates, Eternity and Harmony with nine musicians playing and singing. Confusion was banished. The Fates

set a tree of gold before the Queen, and Eternity invited her to
pluck a branch and undo the spell which, like all other spells, she
alone can undo. The chorus sings:

> Since Knightly valour rescues Dames distressed,
> By Vertuous Dames let charm'd Knights be released.

The Queen pulled a branch from the tree and gave it to a noble-
man, who delivered it to one of the Squires. Out of the air a cloud
descended, revealing six of the Knights; the other six Knights
were then suddenly made to appear out of pillars of gold. They
walked with music to the dancing place. The scene then changed
to London for the masque dances and the revels, after which the
Squires made valedictory speeches and the Knights were carried
away in a barge on the Thames.

The masque depended for its effect on the combined impact
of poetry, music, magic, pageantry and the sense of occasion.
For this reason a bare account of what happened can give little
idea of the aesthetic value of these performances; nor can they
be assessed by reference to any of the components in isolation.
Campion tells us that he published the descriptions and words
of his masques in answer to many requests. For this reason and
because Campion was repeatedly commissioned to write masques
we may assume that they were successful; but there is some
adverse criticism in the letter of a contemporary (F. Chamber-
lain): 'That night was the Lords' Mask, whereof I hear no great
commendation, save only for riches, their devices being long and
tedious, and more like a play than a mask.'[1] It is strange to find
Campion blamed for going too far in the direction of drama, at
which he was a tiro.

Contemporary opinion plays only a small part in determining
the later evaluation or permanence of artistic products; in the
case of the masque, contemporary opinion favoured those features which debased it to the level of pantomime or fashion
parade. But retrospective criticism of an art as occasional in
purpose as the masque is also imperfect, for the emotions and
attitudes expressed in it are often incomprehensible or unacceptable to us; in contrast with Attic and Elizabethan drama, for
example, the masque form has become archaic, a venerable fos-
sil. Nevertheless we can see a better cohesion between the

---

[1] Welsford, op. cit., p. 192.

ingredients of the *Masque in honour of Lord Hayes* than in the
later masques—perhaps because it had no antimasque, a fashion
which was uncongenial to Campion but forced upon him in his
later efforts. Enid Welsford has described the construction of the
Lords' Masque as confused and poor, but finds that it is saved
by its poetry and, presumably, by its staging. Of the *Masque in
honour of the Earl of Somerset* she says that the construction is
worse than usual, and even the lyrics are not very attractive; but
she finds that the work has some interest in showing the tendency
of the masque to turn into mere pantomime. This harsh view is
not shared by Evans,[1] who ranks Campion next to Jonson as a
masque writer—on account of the excellence of his poetry; for it
is this alone which gives the masque something beyond a merely
historical interest.

THE POETRY

Apart from descriptions, stage directions and most of the
dialogue in *Lord Knowles' Entertainment*, the text of all the
masques is in verse, comprising song-lyrics, speeches and dedicatory lines. Not all of this can be described as poetry, but there is
some fine and characteristic writing.

The song-lyrics share many features with those in the song
books—e.g. the interest and variety of rhythm, the frequent
references to music and a lack of visual detail; but few of them
can be taken out of their context, for they refer to episodes in the
masques. More often than in the song books we feel that the
poetry is written expressly for the music and of little account
without it. Sometimes there are weaknesses of design due, perhaps, to hasty composition. Perhaps the most pleasing lyrics are
the dancing songs, such as the dialogue of Silvans and Hours in
the Masque for Lord Hayes, and the fifth song (printed
separately at the end of the masque) with its memorable opening:[2]

> Time, that leads the fatall round,
> Hath made his center in our ground,
> With swelling seas embraced;

[1] *English Masque* (ed. H. A. Evans), Blackie, London, 1897.
[2] Only the music of this song (by M. Lupo) was performed with the
masque, for dancing.

> And there at one stay he rests,
> And with the fates keepes holy feasts,
> With pomp and pastime graced.

But in this, and still more so in most of the other songs, references to the action of the masque deprive the songs of independent life. Individual lines or passages catch the eye, usually on account of varied and subtle word music, as in this:

> Come away; bring thy golden theft,
> Bring, bright Prometheus, all thy lights;
> Thy fires from Heav'n bereft
> Shew now to humane sights.
> Come quickly, come: thy stars to our stars straight present . . .
>
> See how faire, O how faire, they shine,
> What yeelds more pompe beneath the skies?

Sometimes (but rarely) the appeal is to the mind, by reason of a terse or epigrammatic precision: e.g.

> Happie is he whose words can move,
> Yet sweete notes help perswasion . . .

There is, however, nothing in these lyrics to compare with the best poetry of the song books, and too often a happy start is ruined by fulsome compliments or trite comparisons.

The speeches and dialogue are, on the whole, more interesting artistically and as a sample of the kind of verse which Campion wrote when he had no musical setting in mind. They are written for the most part in rhyming couplets with the elegance, the variety and the epigrammatic tension which one might expect from Campion. The opening speech of Night as she burst upon the peaceful, floral scene in the Masque for Lord Hayes is effective and typical:

> Vanish, darke vales; let night in glory shine
> As she doth burn in rage: come, leave our shrine,
> You black-hair'd hours, and guide us with your lights;
> Flora hath wakened wide our drowsy sprights:
> See where she triumphs, see her flowers are throwne,
> And all about the seedes of malice sowne.
> Despightful Flora, ist not enough of griefe
> That Cynthia's robd, but thou must grace the theefe?

Or didst not hear Nights soveraigne Queene complaine
Hymen had stolne a Nimph out of her traine,
And matcht her here, plighted henceforth to be
Loves friend, and stranger to Virginitie?
And mak'st thou sport for this?

The dialogue at the beginning of the Lords' Masque is less
formal and more in the style of Jacobean theatre, but with some
moments of embarrassing naïvety; as when Entheus, released
from the clutches of Mania, speaks to Orpheus: 'Am I free? Is
my affliction vanisht?' and receives this reply:

Too too long,
Alas, good Entheus, hast thou brook't this wrong.
What! number thee with madmen! O mad age,
Sencelesse of thee, and thy celestiall rage . .

Formal speeches were more congenial to Campion's idiom than
the racy dialogue and irony in which Jonson excelled and which
were the life of the antimasque.

The dedicatory verses include one good and melodious poem,
an address to the Reader at the end of the Masque for Lord
Hayes, which is also a fair summary of Campion's limited inten-
tions in the composition of masques:

Neither buskin now, nor bayes
Challenge I: a Ladies prayse
Shall content my proudest hope.
Their applause was all my scope;
And to their shrines properly
Revels dedicated be:
Whose soft eares none ought to pierce
But with smooth and gentle verse.
Let the tragicke Poeme swell,
Raysing raging feendes from hell;
And let Epicke Dactils range
Swelling seas and Countries strange;
Little roome small things containes;
Easy prayse quites easy paines.
Suffer them whose browes do sweat
To gaine honour by the great:
Its enough if men me name
A Retailer of such fame.

The Music

Music was at least as important as poetry in the masque, and it was provided in a great variety of forms, both instrumental and vocal. Bacon, who probably had first hand experience in the productions of masques at Gray's Inn, held strong opinions on the place and quality of music for such occasions: 'Let the Songs be loud and cheerefull, and not chirpings, or pulings. Let the Musicke likewise be sharpe, and loud, and well placed. . . . Severall quires, placed one over against another, and taking the voice antheme wise, give great pleasure.' He also praises dancing to song and acting in song, especially in dialogues.

Campion tells us about the songs, the choruses, the orchestral music, the antiphony of groups of instruments and singers, and the playing of hidden hautboys in the production of his masques; his descriptions (see p. 94) give us a vivid picture of what was happening, but unfortunately nothing remains to show what the orchestral writing was like. There are five songs, two of them by Campion, published at the end of the description of the Masque for Lord Hayes, and reprinted in the Old English Edition in 1889. Another lute song was printed to fill an empty page at the end of the Masque for the Earl of Somerset. Dance tunes from the masques have also survived, but with no orchestration.

J. P. Cutts[1] has drawn attention to a manuscript book in the British Museum containing 138 dance tunes from Jacobean masques, including tunes from Lord Hayes' Masque and from the Lords' Masque. In these only treble and bass part-books appear. The parts are written with time-signature but no bar-lines, and sometimes with no key-signature. The copies are obviously inaccurate, for the two parts cannot be fitted without occasionally changing the note-values, and some accidentals appear to have been omitted in addition to those which the performer would have added in accordance with the convention of *musica ficta*. The tunes are remarkably similar in structure and, when bar-lines are inserted, they are seen to consist of 12 or 13 bars in simple binary form, with self-repeating halves. Musically they are unexciting. Perhaps the best is the one labelled *The Lord Hayes his first Masque* (presumably the first dance):[2]

---

[1] Jacobean Masque and Stage Music, in *Music & Letters*, London (1954), **35**, 185. [2] There is no key-signature in the manuscript.

H

Repeated notes are a feature of the tunes. The music does not seem particularly characteristic of Campion's style, but one can detect in it a weakness which occurs also in some of his lesser lute songs—the tendency to anticipate a note or a chord; as in the following example from the tune inscribed *The Second of the Lords*, where one might wish the F on the third crotchet of the second bar in the bass had not been anticipated:

Of the three songs which survive, the most interesting is undoubtedly *Wooe her and win her* from the Lords' Masque (see Figure 3). The shapely melody is typical of Campion at his nearbest. The opening provides a good example of his rhythmic subtlety; the effect in performance, though the original is barred in duple time, would be something like this:

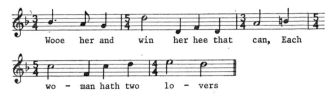

This is sung in the transformation scene while the metamorphosed female statues are being wooed each by two knights. It is a pity that such a charming song cannot be properly understood out of its context, and that the context itself should be so unacceptable.

Now hath Flora rob'd her bowers, from Lord Hayes' Masque, is set for three voices (soprano, tenor and bass) with accompaniment for two 'mean' (i.e. tenor) lutes, a bass lute and a deep bandora. The effect of this combination must have been pleasing,

especially in its context, where Flora and two silvans, soon after
the curtain rises, sing while they scatter flowers from their
baskets on a scene of great splendour. The melody is simple and
smoothly flowing as befits the words. While Campion generally
preferred a homophonic texture, this song shows a genuine
feeling for independent part-writing.

The other song from Lord Hayes' Masque, *Move now with
measured sound*, was sung during the transformation scene, when
the Knights of Phoebus, still in the shape of golden trees, moved
and danced in time to the music. It is set in four parts for two
trebles and two basses, with the same instruments accompanying
as in *Now hath Flora rob'd her bowers*. The tune is straightforward, but musically unexciting.

A. J. Sabol[1] has emphasised the significance of dialogue songs
in Campion's masques; these 'conversation pieces' (the music of
which, unfortunately, is lost) may, in his view, have had some
importance in the development of dramatic music. He also shows
how Campion achieves contrast and variety in Lord Hayes'
Masque not by the use of antimasque but by instrumental
effects. Sabol also discusses the rhythm of dances and dancing
songs; these are described in Sir John Davies' *Orchestra*,[2] where
the language of poetry gives the scene an extraordinary vividness:

> What shall I name those current traverses
> That on a triple dactyl foot do run,
> Close by the ground with sliding passages? . . .
>
> Yet is there one, the most delightful kind,
> A lofty jumping, or a leaping round,
> When arm in arm two dancers are entwined,
> And whirl themselves with strict embracements bound,
> And still their feet an anapaest do sound.

Other composers contributed music to Campion's masques –
Lupo and Thomas Giles for Lord Hayes' Masque, Coperario
and Nicholas Lanier for the Earl of Somerset's Masque. In the
published description of the former it is stated that the songs by
Lupo and Giles were originally written only for dancing, and

---

[1] *Songs and Dances of the Stuart Masque*, Providence, 1959.
[2] *Silver Poets of the Sixteenth Century* (ed. G. Bullett), Dent, London,
1947, p. 331.

Song, made by *Th. Campion*, and fung in the Lords Maske at the *Count Palatines* Marriage, we haue here added, to fill vp thefe emptie Pages.

Ooe her and win her hee that can, Each wo-man
So fhe muft take and leaue a man, Till time more

hath two Lo-uers: This doth *Ioue* to fhew that want makes beau-tie
grace dif-co-uers.   If   faire Women were more fcant, they would be

more refpe-cted.
more affe-cted.

2 Courtſhip and Muſicke ſute with Loue;
  They both are workes of paſſion :
Happy is hee whoſe words can moue,
  Yet ſweet Notes help perſwaſion.
Mixe your words with Muſicke then,
  That they the more may enter :
Bold aſſaults are fit for men,
  That on ſtrange beauties venter.

BASSO.   V.

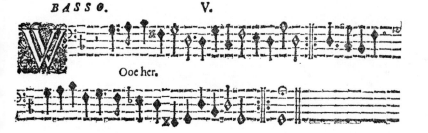

Ooe her.

FINIS.

Fig. 3. A song from *The Lords' Masque*

that words were added so that they could be sung to the lute or viol. There is, in fact, no certainty that the rest of the music (including the dance tunes preserved in the British Museum) was by Campion: for once the poet is named and the composer largely anonymous.

7

POEMS OF
THE LATER SONG BOOKS (1)

THE misnamed First and Second Books of Airs (*Two Bookes of Ayres*) were published together. They are undated, but cannot have appeared before 1612, since they contain an elegy to Prince Henry, who died in November of that year. Like the earlier song-book written in collaboration with Philip Rosseter, this one consists of two groups of twenty-one songs. In a preface to the book Campion says that it contains a few of the many songs which he had written long since, partly at the request of friends, and partly for his own recreation. He had divided them between two books, one 'grave and pious', the other 'amorous and light'. As for the music, it was intended mostly for one voice accompanied by lute or viol, but other vocal parts were provided for those who wished to sing it in parts—and to prevent the improvisation of bystanders which, whether 'true or false, out it must, though to the perverting of the whole harmonie'. As in the preface to his part of Rosseter's Book, Campion likens airs to epigrams, and empha-sises the skill needed in composing them. Though he makes no mystery of his authorship this time, he covers himself by words in defence of publication: 'others taste nothing that comes forth in print, as if Catullus or Martials Epigrammes were the worse for being published.' He also explains the inclusion of sacred and profane works together in one volume, saying (in the dedication of the Second Book) that he wishes to satisfy all tastes, in par-ticular the old with 'pure hymnes, such as the seaventh day loves' and the young with 'weeke-day workes'. These are juxtaposed, like Milton's *L'Allegro* and *Il Penseroso* or Blake's *Songs of Innocence and Experience*, as complementary sides of human life—an arrangement characteristic of Campion's passion for order and balance.

The poems have the variety, brilliance and apparent spon-taneity of those in Rosseter's Book, with more consistent crafts-manship, but with some lapses—especially in the First Book.

Several poems from the earlier collection reappear in revised and obviously improved form. The music, on the other hand, is less varied and memorable than that of the earlier volume, but it shows a trend towards the more homophonic texture which Campion advocates in his late treatise on counterpoint.

THE POEMS

Campion's temperament was more in tune with secular than with religious subjects, but his *First Booke of Ayres* (*Divine and Morall Songs*) is in many ways characteristic. We do not find in these poems the contemplative heights of Vaughan, the ecstasies of Crashaw, the intellectual rigours of Herbert or Donne, the splendours of Milton. Campion, on the other hand, does not disappoint us, as Herrick in his *Noble Numbers* often does, with a lack of wonder and a preoccupation with ritual. His tone is generally calm, and his subjects are varied–as often concerned with the good life as with the worship of God. The words have a quality which, even without the music, suggests song. The influence of Horace and of the Psalms is transformed by Campion's word-magic into shapes of freshness and vitality reminiscent of his secular verse.

The first poem is a prayer for grace, expressed in a series of related images of healing. In the first stanza he addresses God as 'Author of light', begging him to cure his blindness; in the second he calls on Him as 'Fountaine of health' to heal his wound. The images are medical and come as near as the poet ever does to betraying the influence of his other profession, as in the following lines:

> one drop of thy desired grace
> The faint and fading hart can raise.

The blindness which he begs to have cured is spiritual, for he can see 'Sunne and Moone, Starres and underlights', but these sights compared with God are 'mists and darknes'. This symbolic use of darkness and light is naïve and the reverse of that found in some mystical poems where, in Elizabeth Jennings' words, the poet is led into an area which is 'dark with excessive light'–for example Vaughan's lines:

> There is in God (some say)
> A deep but dazzling darkness; as men here
> Say it is late and dusky, because they
> See not all clear.

Campion speaks of no vision, only of the desire for such vision—
or, at least, for the blessings of piety. The language is illuminated
by no surprises or discoveries. Its chief originality is musical,
the pattern of irregular lines repeated in the second stanza—an
arrangement determined by the musical setting, but giving the
poem a peculiar grace which is independent of the music.

The revised version of *The man of life upright* (see R.B.
I, 18) which follows *Author of light* is complementary in subject
and form to the first poem. It is a song in praise of piety and the
good life in which a man 'needes neyther towres, nor armour for
defence' and does not fear 'the horrors of the deepe, and terrors
of the Skies'. The style is unadorned and epigrammatic, with
echoes of the first Psalm and reminders of Horace ('Beatus ille
qui procul negotiis . . .'). The changes in the second version of
the poem are for the better; e.g. the first stanza appears in the
earlier version as follows:

> The man of life upright,
>   Whose guiltlesse hart is free
> From all dishonest deedes,
>   Or thought of vanitie.

This is stripped of redundancy in the second version:

> The man of life upright,
>   Whose chearfull minde is free
> From waight of impious deedes
>   And yoake of vanitee.

Other improvements are the replacement of 'sorrow' by 'sorrows'
('whom hopes cannot delude, nor sorrowes discontent'), and
'good thoughts his onely friends' by 'good thoughts his surest
friends'. The sixth quatrain is strengthened by a change from

> He makes the heav'n his booke,
>   His wisedome heev'nly things

to

> His Booke the Heav'ns hee makes,
>   His wisedome heav'nly things.

In the next poem (*Where are all thy beauties now*) Campion
instances what may happen when beauty usurps the rôle of
goodness. Faded and cold, the former cynosure is now rejected;
but there is comfort in knowing that she, at least, is better than
her flatterers, and will be remembered when they are forgotten.
The form is memorable–strictly metrical tercets with feminine
rhymed endings and an effective delay on the first syllable of
every third line. This breaks the unemphatic flow at a point
where it threatens to become monotonous.

In subtle juxtaposition with this poem, the next one–a metrical
version of Psalm 130–is also in rhyming tercets, but with looser
rhythm, and some metrical ambiguity; e.g. the first line can
receive either six or five stresses:

> Óut of my sóules déapth to thée my crýes have sóunded.

or

> Out of mỳ soules déapth to thée my crýes have sóunded.

As in *Author of light*, there is vividness of form with drabness of
diction, and the same medical image is used:

'Their sinne-sicke soules by him shall be recured.' Medical
images are used again in the poem that follows (*View mee, Lord, a
worke of thine*):

> But my soule still surfets so
>   On the poysoned baytes of sinne,
> That I strange and ugly growe,
>   All is darke and foule within.

There is little poetry in this piece or in the next (*Bravely deckt
come forth, bright day*) which celebrates the defeat of Guy
Fawkes' plot with a jauntiness reminiscent of the songs in the
masques; after a moment of promise ('Death had enter'd in the
gate, And ruine was crept neare the State'), the verse declines
into a stream of cliché and flattery. After this, the beauty and
directness of the seventh poem (*To Musicke bent is my retyred
minde*) brings refreshment. The thought is simple: the poet is
inclined to express his pleasure in music, but now finds no
comfort in transient things:

> All earthly pompe or beauty to expresse,
> Is but to carve in snow, on waves to write.

–a visual image rather unusual in Campion's poems and reminiscent of words in Rosseter's Book (R.B. II, 10):

> My object now must be the aire,
> To write in water words of fire.

As elsewhere, the mention of music evokes an echoing perfection of sound in the poem. There are few epithets, and those are functional. The inspiration is worldly; although 'celestial things' are praised above the visible world, they are presented (as in *Author of light*) with jaded imagery and with little sense of illumination.

Inspired again by music, the next poem (*Tune thy Musicke to thy hart*) has a more epigrammatic style. The plain language and strict metre match the sense of the words (though the general idea is somewhat elusive): worship requires no adornment; therefore artifice and adornment should be avoided in our songs, and the love they protest should be unfeigned. The third stanza, a eulogy of love, is declamatory and seems, in a way, separate from the rest. Returning to the form and meditative style of the seventh poem, the ninth (*Most sweet and pleasing are thy wayes*) echoes and then departs from the psalms in comparing the ways of God with meadows, crystal streams and flowers unvisited by the profane, the violent–and the carnivorous; a place where doves and lambs are found, but no vultures, wolves or lion:

> The darksome Desart all such beasts contaynes,
> Not one of them in Paradice remaynes.

Pursuing the logical implications of his image in the manner of the metaphysicals, Campion moves away from the decorum of the Psalms or Genesis to the naïve symbolism of the bestiaries.

Few poets use such a variety of forms, and this variety is matched by the consistency of style and form within each of the poems. After the uninflected simplicity of the ninth poem comes a poem which is strangely and consistently inflected:

> Wise men patience never want:
> Good men pitty cannot hide;
> Feeble spirits onely vant
> Of revenge, the poorest pride:
> Hee alone, forgive that can,
> Beares the true soule of a man.

It has the air of experiment, like the Sapphics of Rosseter's Book (R.B. I, 21), with perhaps a wistful emulation of Latin syntax. At times the language is uncouth (e.g. 'Kindnesse growne is, lately, colde'), and sometimes inflection conceals the meaning (e.g. 'All so thrives his gentle rayes, where on humane love displayes', which is best construed when 'his gentle rayes' is placed after 'displayes'). The poem cannot be counted a success, but it is interesting to find in the third stanza an indictment of the cynicism and immorality of the times that reminds one of Wordsworth ('Plain living and high thinking are no more').

The eleventh poem (*Never weather-beaten Saile*) is one of Campion's most famous lyrics, in its freshness and simplicity the complete antithesis of the twisted lines of the previous poem. The thought is slight, but the imagery is strikingly visual and there is one of Campion's favourite medical images in the second quatrain:

> Cold age deafes not there our eares, nor vapour dims our eyes.

The magic lies largely in the word music of phrases which also carry an evocative image–especially the first two lines, and the expansion of the long third line of each stanza which expresses first the yearning for escape and flight, and then the glory of heaven presented with the naïve assumptions of childhood. Another hymn follows (*Lift up to heav'n, sad wretch, thy heavy spright*), less memorable but with a striking and euphonious final couplet:

> Strive then, and hee will help; call him he'll heare:
> The Sonne needes not the Fathers fury feare.

The thirteenth poem is remarkable for its image of a man who walks blindfold through danger and escapes injury. The form and language are prophetic of George Herbert:

> Loe, when backe mine eye,
>   Pilgrim-like, I cast,
> What fearefull wayes I spye,
> Which, blinded, I securely past?
>
> But now heav'n hath drawne
>   From my browes that night;
> As when the day doth dawne,
> So cleares my long imprison'd sight.

Straight the caves of hell,
  Drest with flowres I see:
Wherein false pleasures dwell,
  That, winning most, most deadly be . . . .

Simplicity and an absence of adornment are the correct accompaniment of a theme in which the subject is sufficient cause for surprise, and in the transparent but metrically rigid pattern of these quatrains Campion comes as near as he ever does to conveying a mystical intuition. Something is lost in the three remaining stanzas, but the poem as a whole has consistency and tension.

The metrical version of Psalm 137 (*As by the streames of Babilon*) follows the sense of the original closely, but with exaggeration of its savagery ('Blest shall they be thy babes that take And 'gainst the stones dash out their braines'); the language is inflected sometimes to the point of absurdity (e.g. O *Salem*, thee when I forget, Forget his skill may my right hand). There is characteristic musical imagery when he prays that his tongue may cleave to the roof of his mouth 'if, when all my joys are sung, *Jerusalem* be not the ground'. In spite of felicitous phrases, the poem does not come to life. Still less alive, the next poem (*Sing a song of joy*) consists of a succession of undigested fragments of loose translation from Psalm 136 in strict metre that seems incongruous with the content of the psalm; unlike the same metre used in poem 13, it fails in this poem to communicate tension and excitement. Questions and statements are interspersed with little care. In the next poem lofty sentiments are smothered by triteness of diction and a sing-song triviality of form (Seeke heav'n earely, seeke it late: True faith still findes an open gate); but the poem ends with a fine couplet.

In the seventeenth poem (*Come, chearfull day*) Campion returns to his best meditative and epigrammatic manner. The form is one which Campion (uncharacteristically) used several times, but the poems in this form include some of his best writing (e.g. *When thou must home to shades of under ground* and *The sypres curten of the night is spread*). The two stanzas are nicely counterpoised; in the first he welcomes day as 'part of my life', but sees how in its fading light

Part of my life doth still depart with thee.

In the second stanza he regrets the life lost in sleep but sees how that 'fayned death' revives the soul's temporary residence. Each stanza is knit with the concise and memorable refrain:

> So ev'ry day we live a day wee dye.

The eighteenth song (*Seeke the Lord, and in his wayes persever*) is written for the tune which Campion had used in his earlier song *Followe thy faire sunne* (R.B. I, 4). The poem is undistinguished, a confused sequence of cliché and mixed metaphor in which man is exhorted to fly as an eagle because the steep hill is high, so that he may there be crowned with glory and see such sights 'that worldly thoughts shall by their beames be drowned'. This may have been deliberate—an illustration of the 'meere confusion' he wishes to leave behind; but the advantage of this technique in a description of heaven is doubtful. The metre is not quite identical with that of *Followe thy faire sunne*; the two extra syllables in the second line of each stanza make its iambic start less pleasing after the feminine ending of the first line: e.g.

> Whén with glóry thére thy brówes are crówned,
> New jóys só shall abóund in thée . . .

In contrast with such apparently careless versification the matching of the words to the music is meticulous, including such felicities as the last line of each stanza in which (as in *Followe thy faire sunne*) a climbing figure is matched by an appropriate image:

> Then striving gaine the top, and triumph ever.

> That all who taste it are from death restored.

The imagery of Darkness and Light which Campion used so often is used similarly in the two poems:

> Til her kind beames that black to brightnes turneth (R.B. I, 4)
> That worldly thoughts shall by their beames be drowned (I, 18)

The other cure for confusion—activity—is much more successfully invoked in the nineteenth poem (*Lighten, heavy hart, thy spright*). There is a reminder of Spenserian allegory in the references to the cave of sloth, and Campion's own epigrammatic strain flashes out:

> Yeeld thy brest some living light;
> The man that nothing doth is dead,

(Compare 'All doe not all things well', in III, 12.)

The security and happiness of country folk is contrasted with cares of court life in the next poem, which avoids sentimentality by a naïve directness, a lack of ornament and an unusual wealth of visual images. There is a foretaste of Milton's *L'Allegro* in some of the lines:

> Skip and trip it on the greene,
> And help to chuse the Summer Queene:
> Lash out, at a Country Feast,
> Their silver penny with the best.
>
> Well can they judge of nappy Ale,
> And tell at large a Winter tale;
> Climbe up to the Apple loft,
> And turne the Crabs till they be soft.

The poem has some affinity with the third poem in Rosseter's Book I (*I care not for these ladies*), but without the sophistication and irony of the earlier work.

An elegy for Prince Henry (*All lookes be pale*), placed at the end of this book, is a sad anticlimax. These trite, occasional verses seem to belong properly to the *Songs of Mourning*, and presumably they found their place in the *First Booke of Ayres* because Campion himself composed the music.

The *Second Booke of Ayres* (*Light Conceits of Lovers*) is inscribed to Henry, Lord Clifford, son of the Earl of Cumberland for whom the *Divine and Morall Songs* were written. In these poems Campion returns to his natural element and the level of artistry is more consistently high.

The first poem follows logically, with its reference to the folly of 'making a God of Love', from the *Divine Songs*, and illustrates many of Campion's best qualities:

> Vaine men, whose follies make a God of Love,
> Whose blindnesse beauty doth immortall deeme;
> Prayse not what you desire, but what you prove,
> Count those things good that are, not those that seeme:
> I cannot call her true that's false to me,
> Nor make of women more than women be.

How faire an entrance breakes the way to love!
How rich of golden hope and gay delight!
What hart cannot a modest beauty move?
Who, seeing cleare day once, will dreame of night?
Shee seem'd a Saint, that brake her faith with mee,
But prov'd a woman as all other be.

So bitter is their sweet, that true content
Unhappy men in them may never finde:
Ah, but without them none; both must consent,
Else uncouth are the joys of eyther kinde.
Let us then prayse their good, forget their ill:
Men must be men, and women women still.

The poem is written in two 'voices', one speaking abstractions
in the first four lines of each stanza, the other recounting a
personal history in the rhyming couplets at the end of each stanza.
Each voice conveys what is, in effect, a separate poem, the thread
being carried from one stanza to the next. This 'polyphony' is
enhanced by the opposing moods of the two voices, one enjoining
common sense ('count those things good that are, not those that
seeme'), the other confessing defeat ('true content Unhappy men
in them may never finde'). At one moment the tone is curiously
prophetic of the Augustan period:

What hart cannot a modest beauty move?

At another moment the tone recalls Donne:

She seem'd a Saint, that brake her faith with mee,
But prov'd a woman as all other be.

The fatalism of the final couplet is true Campion and reminiscent
of *My sweetest Lesbia* (R.B. I, 1), in which the poet invites his
friends to enjoy themselves at his funeral.

There is a backward glance at the third of the *Divine Songs* in
the next poem, which recounts the commonplace of rejection by
a beauty whose smile 'chained' him—and no wonder, since she is
a goddess; yet who would expect deception from such a being?
The metaphor of divinity in this poem, as in the first, is like an
echo of the *First Booke of Ayres*. The two stanzas are nicely
balanced, the first moving from the key of disillusion, through

remembered pleasure to an ecstasy of worship; the second starting from this point and returning through memory of unkindness to the opening key of disillusion:

> No wonder if I languish
> Through burden of my smart;
> It is no common anguish
> From Paradice to part.

In the next poem, a direct sequel of the second, the poet continues addressing his heart ('Harden now thy tyred hart, with more than flinty rage'), commanding it to turn a cold eye now upon his inconstant mistress. The language, however, is less functional than in the previous poem, and there are many stale epithets (*'flinty* rage', *'constant* griefe', *'bright* houres', *'carelesse* tresses', *'pretty* talke'). Unlike the previous poem, too, it suffers rather than gains from being designed for music, requiring in the last line of each stanza a distortion of speech rhythm

> Such a time there was, God wot, but such shall never be:
> Too oft, I feare, thou wilt remember me.

If the last line is read simply as an iambic pentameter it is ill-matched against the preceding five lines of precisely thirteen syllables and seven stresses.

A sudden outburst of relief and exuberance, the fourth poem moves with simplicity song:

> That which I long despair'd to be,
> To her I am, and shee to mee.

Nevertheless, it clings to the 'divine' imagery of the earlier poems:

> Both are immortall and divine:
> Since I am hers, and she is mine.

'Divine' imagery is continued in the fifth poem ('Where shee her sacred bowre adornes, the Rivers clearely flow'). With hopes revived by the moment of success (fourth poem), he carries the argument of the second poem one stage further in accepting a new rebuff:

> And though not in her bowre, yet I
> Shall in her temple rest.

I

The euphuistic exaggeration of this standpoint makes the poem unconvincing. Its imagery is sometimes trite, occasionally inaccurate: e.g.

> Her Sunne-like beauty shines so fayre,
>   Her Spring can never fade:
> Who then can blame the life that strives
>   To harbour in her shade?

There is a moment of felicity in the third stanza, when he finds some of his mistress' beauty his own creation:

> Her roses with my prayers shall spring;
>   And when her trees I praise,
> Their boughs shall blossome . . .

and a characteristic (though dilute) touch of epigram in the fourth stanza.

The dilemma is more candidly expressed when, in the next poem, he dares not disclose his love, in case she leaves him ('If not happy, safe Ile be'), and yet cannot endure the thwarting of desire ('A wound long hid growes past recure'–the favourite medical image). The thought becomes more involved: she is wise, and therefore knows how beauty stimulates desire; no matter how strong her will against it, she will be sought if she is fair; then follows a cryptic conclusion:

> When true theeves use falsehood well,
>   As they are wise they will be caught.

which suggests an ambiguity (not altogether successful) in the use of the word 'wise'.

Another interlude of relaxation follows (cf. II, 4)

> Give beauty all her right,
> Shee's not to one forme tyed;
> Each shape yeelds faire delight,
> Where her perfections 'bide.
> Hellen, I grant, might pleasing be;
> And Ros'mond was as sweet as shee.

The poem is simple, yet marred by careless composition in the second stanza.

To escape from returning fears and jealousies which make his love 'diseased like a sicke man's rest' he longs, in the next poem, to live alone with his beloved. The poem which starts with this cry of longing and proceeds through questionings to an epigrammatic conclusion is neatly balanced, and the couplet of longer lines sounds well after the quatrain of short lines:

> How oft have wee ev'n smilde in teares,
>   Our fond mistrust repenting?
> As snow when heavenly fire appeares,
>   So melts loves hate relenting.
> Vexed kindnesse soone fals off and soone returneth:
> Such a flame the more you quench, the more it burneth.

The woman laments her desertion in the ninth poem, searching for pity with tears relieved by irony:

> Oh! if such a Saint there be,
> Some hope yet remaines for me.

The situation, analogous to that of R.B. I, 5, is told with less emotion and spontaneity, and with more intellectual probing.

The first six lines of the tenth poem ('What harvest halfe so sweet is') are taken without alteration from the second stanza of R.B. I, 7, and followed by a quatrain more polished in metre and sense than those which appear in the earlier version. In the second stanza the image of the Dove—a creature fervent in kisses but quite harmless—is mildly grotesque and out of keeping with the sustained harvest imagery of the first stanza. The final quatrain is virtually a précis of R.B. I, 1 (*My sweetest Lesbia*).

Several of the characteristic felicities of Campion appear in the next poem ('Sweet, exclude mee not')—a limpid and varied music with an effective refrain, a consistency of image, a mingling of the lyrical and the epigrammatic. The lover begs his betrothed to let him in:

> Tenants, to fulfill their Land-lord's pleasure,
>   Pay their rent before the quarter:
> 'Tis my case, if you it rightly measure;
>   Put mee not then off with laughter.

The ambiguity of his position is represented in the image of law:

> All thy maiden doubts Law hath decided.

but later

> Why were dores in loves despight devised?
> Are not Lawes enough restrayning?

There is a reminder of sweet Bessie (R.B. I, 8) in

> Women are most apt to be surprised
> Sleeping, or sleepe wisely fayning.

This mellowness is carried over into *The peacefull Westerne Winde*, a poem in which the approach of Spring is hailed in three stanzas of smiling (if unadventurous) euphony, with at times a foretaste of Blake:

> See how the morning smiles
> On her bright easterne hill,
> And with soft steps beguiles
> Them that lie slumbring still.

In the fourth stanza a conventional complaint is poured out with little conviction, like a peace offering.

In the thirteenth poem complaint is seasoned with irony: only she who gives him no favours, delights his eyes; but beauty is frail; therefore let him survey all her looks that he may (echoing Ronsard)

> Fill the world with envyed bookes:
>
> Which when after ages view,
>   All shall wonder and despaire,
> Woman to finde man so true,
>   Or man a woman halfe so faire,

More enigmatic, the fourteenth poem stays on a semi-abstract psychological plane and reaches its sharpest definition in the couplet

> The same thing I seeke and flie,
> And want that which none would denie.

The 'thing' haunts, elusive, disturbing, waiting to be challenged, like a ghost and yet tangible.

The more tangible psychology of the fifteenth poem (*So many loves have I neglected*) is that of the woman who has rejected many lovers and now finds the tables turned, a further variation of the theme already worked over in I, 3 and II, 9. The central idea is, characteristically, a paradox:

> O happy men, whose hopes are licenc'd
> To discourse their passion,
> While women are confin'd to silence,
> Loosing wisht occasion.
> Yet our tongues then theirs, men say,
> Are apter to be moving,

There is a tendency towards assonance in place of rhyme (e.g. 'licenc'd' and 'silence', 'wooed' and 'vowed', 'strangenesse' and 'plainenesse'), a departure from regularity which gives a new liveliness to the verse.

The poem ends with a confession:

> Maydes, I see, are never blest
> That strange be but for fashion.

and the next poem is the man's reply:

> Though your strangenesse frets my hart,
> Yet may not I complaine:
> You perswade me, 'tis but Art,
> That secret love must faine.

With bitter irony he wishes that he were his rival, for while, in her words, he holds her heart, they (the rivals) hold her hand:

> Is this faire excusing? O, no, all is abusing.

Another lyrical interlude in this struggle of wits follows:

> Come away, arm'd with loves delights,
> Thy spritefull graces bring with thee,
> When loves longing fights,
> They must the sticklers be.
> Come quickly, come, the promis'd houre is wel-nye spent,
> And pleasure being too much deferr'd looseth her best content . . .

The seductive rhythms of this poem, varied from line to line, are refreshingly contrasted with the regular and sometimes metronomic rhythm of several poems which come before it. Even without music, the lines have the quality of song. 'Stickler' here means a duellist's second, and lines 3 and 4 would then imply:

when Desire fights a duel (as, for example, in the previous poem), Beauty and Wit must come to her aid as seconds.

The duel continues in the eighteenth poem (*Come, you pretty false-ey'd wanton*), but with victory in sight, her cries are smothered first in kisses, which he describes with his favourite harvest image:

> Such a harvest never was,
>> So rich and full of pleasure,
> But 'tis spent as soone as reapt,
>> So trustlesse is loves treasure.

When this weapon is exhausted, he brings his second weapon to the duel,

> And when you cry'd, then would I laugh.

until, victorious, he lives her servant, and she (as in R.B. I, 10), ironically, his saint.

The woman speaks again in the nineteenth poem in which metrical ambiguity seems to echo an ambivalence of content. The gist is expressed in Campion's best epigrammatic vein:

> A secret love or two I must confesse
>> I kindly welcome for change in close playing,
> Yet my deare husband I love ne'erthelesse . . .

> The more a spring is drawne the more it flowes,
>> No Lampe lesse light retaines by lightning others:
> Is hee a looser his losse that nere knowes? . . .

> Wise Archers beare more than one shaft to field.

There is something like mania in the twentieth poem when he jumbles images in a reckless unvisual description of his mistress:

> Her rosie cheekes, her ever smiling eyes,
> Are Spheares and beds where Love in triumph lies.

Among the images are several lifted from his section of Rosseter's Book: e.g.

> Her lookes inflame, yet cold as Ice is shee.

In the last poem he returns to the more habitual air of calm resignation. The stanzas are neatly balanced and each ends with a memorable couplet.

> O bitter griefe, that exile is become
> Reward for faith, and pittie deafe and dumbe.
>
> Oh wretched me, that my chiefe joy should breede
> My onely griefe and kindnesse pitty neede!

8

POEMS OF
THE LATER SONG BOOKS (2)

THE *Third and Fourth Bookes of Ayres*, like the first and second, were published together and again dedicated, respectively, to a father and a son. There is no date on the title-page, but Campion's dedicatory verses to Sir Thomas Monson, which refer to his old patron's recent release from prison, show that the book was published in or after 1617. From a reference in the dedication to 'these youth-born ayres' it is clear that they were written or conceived long before the book appeared. Two poems in the fourth book are revised versions of poems in *A Booke of Ayres*. Campion's style and preoccupations in the third and fourth books are much the same as they were in the earlier publication, and the arrangement of the poems in short sequences related in subject matter and diversified in form is also reminiscent of that work. In the later books, however, there is more variety of form and more consistency of craftsmanship–as shown, for example, in the revised versions of the earlier poems.

The third book begins with a woman's complaint at desertion by one who 'absent hath both love and mee forgot'; without introspection or self-pity she languishes wryly 'for him that can breake vowes but not returne'. The complaint by the man in the second poem shows him isolated, unhearing and putting on an appearance of cynical detachment:

> False, then farewell for ever:
> Once false proves faithful never.

Written with ungarnished simplicity, the poem shows little thought or development, and its moment of epigram has the air of folk wisdom:

> True love abides to th' houre of dying:
> False love is ever flying.

In the third poem, written in 'fourteeners', a similar vein of simplicity conceals more subtle thought: 'Were my hart as some mens are, thy errours would not move me', he says, but love makes him see and speak; enemies who pick on one's faults are better friends than the obsequious guest who pretends to see no evil; in general, 'Hidden mischiefe to conceale in State, and Love is treason'.

The answer to this—that no-one can believe what 'some men' say—is taken up from the woman's angle in the fourth poem: simplicity, they call it, but others might call such scepticism good sense:

> Love they make a poore blinde childe,
> But let none trust such as hee:
> Rather then to be beguil'd,
> Ever let me simple be.

Driven by self-pity to apathy and 'griefe that knowes nor cause, nor cure', the man in poem 5 reaches out for some cure, some action that 'alone makes the soule blest'. The verse-form, quatrains with lines of diminishing length, is appropriate, suggesting change of mood: but the diction is colourless and unmemorable.

In the sixth poem there is complexity of thought and an indirectness of expression that reminds one of metaphysical poetry. The mixture of alliterative euphony and harshness (from juxtaposition of two 'thats') in the first line is consistent with the perplexity and contradiction of the matter in this poem:

> Why presumes thy pride on that that must so private be?

He taxes her with being so proud of her beauty that she would let it become common property; but beauty fades after much handling, and (paradoxically) she will seem fairer if her beauty is reserved for one man. The paradox is complementary to the 'cruell hate of that which sweetest is', the subject of the previous poem. Campion's gifts are not seen at their best in dialectical exercises of this sort; his medium is happier where the impact is immediate, as in the seventh poem which offers a typical fatalistic account of love's dilemma.

> Kinde are her answeres,
>   But her performance keeps no day;
> Breaks time, as dancers
>   From their own Musicke when they stray;

The straying, however, is beyond human control:

> There is no wisedome
> Can alter ends, by Fate prefixt.
> O why is the good of man with evill mixt?
> Never were days yet cal'd two,
> But one night went betwixt.

When Campion gives the theme of love a rest, while still brooding on misfortune, he sometimes achieves a peculiar concentration and timelessness, as in *The Sypres curten of the night* (R.B. I, 9), and in the eighth poem of this book:

> O griefe, O spight, to see poore Vertue scorn'd,
> Truth far exil'd, False arte lov'd, Vice ador'd,
> Free Justice sold, worst causes best adorned,
> Right cast by Powre, Pittie in vaine implor'd!
>   O who in such an age could wish to live,
>   When none can have or hold, but such as give?
>
> O times! O men! to Nature rebels growne,
> Poore in desert, in name rich, proud of shame;
> Wise, but in ill! Your stiles are not your owne,
> Though dearely bought, honour is honest fame.
>   Old Stories onely, goodnesse now containe,
>   And the true wisedome that is just, and plaine.

This generalised distress is more moving than concrete but rhetorical situations that recur in other poems; for example, the ninth of this book, where an epigram ('He that must dye is better dead') is swamped by mellifluous commonplace. Quite different is the tenth poem, in which Campion's functional use of metre and ironic comment are well illustrated. The poem is a dialogue, each stanza consisting of three self-pitying lines (alexandrines) from the male speaker, followed by two sprightly anapaestic lines from the female, the two groups being linked by rhyme. The effect is striking, and the quickened tempo of the anapaestic couplets reminds one of the music (but not the poem) in the last couplet of each stanza in *Vaine men whose follies make a God of love* (II, 1):

> Breake now, my heart, and dye! Oh no, she may relent.
> Let my despaire prevayle! O stay, hope is not spent.

> Should she now fixe one smile on thee, where were despaire?
> The losse is but easy, which smiles can repayre.
> A stranger would please thee, if she were as fayre.

If smiles and kindnesses can repair loss in the tenth poem, in the eleventh they can overthrow tempests. Like the moods of the sea, so those of women are determined by nature. Deceit and beauty are both traitors to love,

> Yet doe we rather wish, what ere befall,
> To have fayre women false then none at all.

The poem that follows (*Now winter nights enlarge*) is an interlude, but it keeps a thread of continuity with the mood of its forerunner:

> Though Love and all his pleasures are but toyes,
> They shorten tedious nights.

The lines of six syllables are broken harmoniously at the end of each stanza by a longer penultimate line, that also interrupts the catalogue of wintry blessings.

The seductive power of the voice, either in speech or in song, is a recurring enthusiasm of Campion's poetry, and in the thirteenth poem the lover implores his mistress to wake up so that he may enjoy her speech, that 'oracle which none can counterfeit'. A hierarchy is outlined in which men surpass the beasts and outshine each other by virtue of speech, 'the best of graces'. Each stanza opens with a couplet of fourteeners and has a singsong regularity that weakens its emotional impact and makes it less memorable than, for example, *When to her lute Corrina sings*, a poem with which it shares some imagery.

The fourteenth poem praises woman as angel in the house:

> If weary, they prepare us rest; if sicke, their hand attends us;
> When with griefe our hearts are prest, their comfort best
>   befriends us:
> Sweet or sowre, they willing goe to share what fortune sends us.

Euphonious and serene, the lines follow each other with little sense of development or organisation; the images are clear and pleasing, but well worn. Nor does the next poem tell us anything that has not been told many times, but its formal simplicity (of heroic couplets with end-stopped lines) and its epigrammatic directness give it an immediate appeal. There are reminders of other poems – e.g. lines 5 and 6 look back to the eleventh poem of R.B. I (*Faire, if you expect admiring*), and line 13 is reminiscent of the tenth poem in that book. Especially characteristic is the paradox expressed in these couplets:

> Prayers move the heav'ns but finde no grace with you;
> Yet in your lookes a heavenly forme I view:
> Then will I pray againe, hoping to finde,
> As well as in your lookes, heav'n in your minde.

When Campion's female characters speak for themselves, they usually plead as innocent victims of a rapacious male (e.g. R.B. I, 5; II, 9; III, 4). In the sixteenth poem, however, the female voice is that of a siren, luring the clueless youth to an ecstasy of love from which he can't escape even when his rivals are suddenly preferred. The couplet of long lines followed by a quatrain of short ones is well suited to the cat-and-mouse fortunes of the poem. The verse is clever and accomplished, but less magical than that of the song which follows:

> Shall I come, sweet Love, to thee,
>   When the ev'ning beames are set?
> Shall I not excluded be?
>   Will you finde no fained lett?
> Let me not, for pitty, more,
> Tell the long houres at your dore.

Magic of another sort is invoked in the eighteenth poem to melt his mistress's heart, and conveyed by subtleties of assonance and alliteration:

> Thrice tosse these Oaken ashes in the ayre,
> Thrice sit thou mute in this inchanted chayre;
> And thrice three times tye up this true loves knot,
> And murmur soft, shee will, or shee will not.

The lover's situation in this poem is complementary to that of the fifteenth, in which he begs his mistress to cure his pain with one touch of grace; here she uses her art to thwart his magic:

> In vaine are all the charms I can devise:
> She hath an Arte to breake them with her eyes,

When at last, in the nineteenth poem, he is accepted, it remains uncertain whether she wants his love, his service or his worship; so to ensure the victory he offers to gratify any or all of these wishes. The sophistication of this poem is nicely balanced by the naïve street cries of the next one:

> Fire, fire, fire, fire.
> Loe here I burne in such desire
> That all the teares that I can straine
> Out of mine idle empty braine
> Cannot allay my scorching paine.

In a frenzy he calls the rivers and seas to put out the fire, but they fall back, and only the rain helps him and saves the world from a holocaust! Yet in the poem that follows he reflects wistfully on Arcadian impossibility:

> O sweet delight, O more than humane blisse,
> With her to live that ever loving is;
> To heare her speake, whose words so well are plac't
> That she by them, as they in her are grac't.

Few poets have so repeatedly stressed the seductive virtues of speech.

The philosophy which allows a man to prefer 'fayre women false than none at all' (III, 11) is again expressed in poem 22, where he refuses to see 'those little staines in youth', accepting such hazards as a fair price for kindness. In any case, human nature cannot be transformed:

> Wilde borne be wilde still, though by force made tame.

The poem is complementary to its forerunner and resembles it in form and in epigrammatic lucidity. In spite of verbal grace and a prophetic hint of Shelley ('Love loves no delay; thy sight, The more enjoyed, the more divine') the poem that follows (number 23) seems to lack substance and purpose after the more thoughtful poems that precede it. With poem 24 we return to the crisp, epigrammatic style: here (cf. II, 1) we find a sort of 'contrapuntal' independence of opening quatrains and closing couplets of each stanza. The philosophy is that of the disenchanted lover who accepts human frailty, his own included:

> Yet no Art or Caution can
> Growne affections easily change;
> Use is such a Lord of Man
> That he brookes worst what is strange.
> Better never to be blest
> Than to loose all at the best.

The final couplet is the antithesis of Tennyson's more famous lines:

> 'Tis better to have loved and lost
> Than never to have loved at all.

Another variation on the theme of disenchantment (poem 25) has an ironic gesture:

> Sleepe, angry beauty, sleep, and feare not me.
> For who a sleeping Lyon dares provoke?
> It shall suffice me here to sit and see
> Those lips shut up that never kindely spoke.
> What sight can more content a lovers minde
> Then beauty seeming harmlesse, if not kinde?

Then, returning to the image of spells, he takes comfort in the thought that his words have charmed her to sleep, and that sleep may plead his case.

The fourteeners of poem 26 are rigid and formal, but there is a melodious grace in the choice of word and image, a mingling of song and sense, of the lyrical and the epigrammatic which makes this piece particularly memorable:

> All is heav'n that you behold, and all your thoughts are blessed;
> But no Spring can want his Fall, each Troylus has his Cresseid.

This might be the worldly-wise father schooling an adolescent son; but the cynicism is broken by a ray of skittish hope:

> Yet be just and constant still; Love may beget a wonder,
> Not unlike a Summers frost, or Winters fatall thunder.

More pearls of fatherly wisdom follow in the next poem, this time addressed to the girl:

> Never love unlesse you can
> Beare with all the faults of man:
> Men sometimes will jealous bee,
> Though but little cause they see . . . .

With jealousy goes the ritual of dissembling and paying court to other beauties, and there must be time for male company and an escape from chatter.

This thread is picked up in the twenty-eighth poem:

> An houre with thee I care not to converse

It is a response—half pitying, half ironic—to the petulance of such poems as the twenty-fifth. The angry beauty would gladly silence her over-zealous lover 'and yeeld some little grace' to quiet him. The thought of yielding to his suit fills her with a confusion of visual images quite unusual in Campion's writing:

> The grove is charg'd with thornes and the bold bryer,
> Gray Snakes the meadowes shrowde in every place:
> A yellow Frog, alas, will fright me so,
> As I should start and tremble as I goe.

The solution has some features reminiscent of Donne:

> Since then I can on earth no fit roome finde,
> In heaven I am resolv'd with you to meete . . .
> A heavenly meeting one day wee shall have,
> But never, as you dreame, in bed, or grave.

The last poem of the book is an answer to this in Campion's best epigrammatic manner, and it concludes the sequence with a fitting gesture:

> Shall I then hope when faith is fled?
>   Can I seeke love when hope is gone?
> Or can I live when Love is dead?
>   Poorely hee lives, that can love none.
>   Her vowes are broke, and I am free;
>   Shee lost her faith in loosing mee . . .

The reference to faith, hope and love in this poem—featureless clichés when taken out of context—seem appropriate and functional when the poem is read as part of the sequence.

An address to the Reader at the beginning of the *Fourth Booke of Ayres* contains some typical comments: 'The Apothecaries have Bookes of Gold, whose leaves being opened are so light as that they are subject to be shaken with the least breath, yet rightly handled, they serve both for ornament and use; such are light Ayres.' These classical virtues are well illustrated by many of the poems that follow. As in the previous books, there is much subtlety in the succession of harmonising and contrasting metrical patterns, but though there are some short sequences, there are more poems that stand apart from their neighbours in this book.

After a tentative opening the book comes to life with aphoristic brilliance; e.g. this in poem 2:

> Some rais'd to rich estates in this time are,
> That held their hopes to mine inferiour farre:
> Such, scoffing mee, or pittying me, say thus,
> Had hee not lov'd, he might have liv'd like us.

or this in poem 3:

> Men that doe noble things all purchase glory:
> One man for one brave Act has[1] prov'd a story:
> But if that one tenne thousand Dames o'ercame,
> Who would record it, if not to his shame?

The moralising is seasoned with wit and paradox, as in poem 4:

> Who can usurp heav'ns light alone?
> Stars were not made to shine on one!

or

> He that a true embrace will finde,
> To beauties faults must still be blinde.

The long, internally rhyming lines of the fifth poem break down naturally into stanzas of shorter lines:

> Ev'ry Dame
> Affects good fame,
>   What ere her doings be,
> But true prayse
> Is Vertues Bayes
>   Which none may weare but she.

The dry, syllabic rhythm is appropriate for the detached social comment of this piece, some of it ageless; e.g. this note on fashion:

> Now such new found toyes are sold, these women to disguise,
> That before the yeare growes old the newest fashion dyes.

> [1] The text reads 'have'.

This is another hymn in praise of 'plain living and high thinking' (cf. R.B. I, 3 and III, 8), and a renunciation of extravagance:

That the wives in silkes may flow, at ebbe the Good-men stand.

The simplicity of the song (No. 6) that follows brings a pleasant relief in form and content. The image of a tree in the second stanza is effective and unusual:

Alas, how soone is this love growne
To such a spreading height in me
As with it all must shadowed be!

The subtlety of this is shown by juxtaposition with the image of light in the previous stanza:

O why invented Nature light?
Was it alone for beauties sake?

By implication, beauty ensures its own eclipse by creating love, which casts everything (including beauty) into the shadow.

Plant imagery is continued in the famous seventh song (*There is a Garden in her face*). Here the imagery is conceptual rather than visual – if we picture the image it becomes ludicrous: nevertheless, the lyric is pleasing and popular – not (as in some non-visual images of Donne) because of its audacity or extravagance, but because of a song-like quality, a strange memorability of phrase that challenges the opposing temptation to laughter. The mood of song is evoked without the music, and visual ineptitudes pass unnoticed (e.g. the brows 'like bended bowes' which threaten with piercing frowns to kill all who attempt to kill the 'sacred cherries'). Less successful is the naïve myth of the eighth poem, in which Midas remains unmoved by Apollo singing the motions of the spheres but is transported by Pan piping the praises of cattle, sheep and 'more of this churlish kinde'; but in this poem the words speak rather than sing.

A blend of the sensuous and the ironic pervades the ninth poem. 'Young and simple though I am', it begins, recalling Amaryllis, the nut-brown maid of Rosseter's book (R.B. I, 3), but the simplicity is affected. She finds a heat

Like thirstlonging, that doth bide
Ever on my weaker side,
Where they say my heart doth move.

K

The linked association of the left side with weakness and with
love is followed by other subtleties–the innate female strength
that feigns weakness or hesitancy, as in

> As good 'twere a thing were past,
> That must needes be done at last

and the final sophisticated jab:

> Yet nor Churle, nor silken Gull,
> Shall my Mayden blossome pull:
> Who shall not I soone can tell;
> Who shall, would I could as well:
>   This I know, whoere hee be,
>   Love hee must, or flatter me.

Echoing the last line of this poem, the lover in the tenth poem
sings in Campion's most melodious and unsophisticated manner:

> Love me or not, love her I must or dye;
> Leave me or not, follow her needs must I.

Here, as so often, the peculiar word rhythms are determined by
the musical setting. Being poet as well as composer, Campion
has produced the rare combination of words and music neither
of which suffers from having to meet the requirements of the
other; the speech rhythms fall as though by accident into the
musical pattern of the song. The regular alternation of couplets
with this biphasic rhythm and simple heroic couplets gives the
poem a kind of pendulum movement which echoes the oscillations of mood in the poem. These oscillations are derided in the
eleventh poem:

> What meanes this folly, now to brave it so,
> And then to use submission?

The epigrammatic style predominates and gives at least one
memorable line ('Though Bryers breed Roses, none the Bryer
affect'), but in other lines the tone is flat and moralistic, with
little development of image or idea. The twelfth poem is more
successful; in answer to the woman's cynical demand for flattery
(poem 9), the male participant in this game of chess scores a
moral, if somewhat priggish, advantage:

> Love forbid that through dissembling I should thrive,
> Or in praysing you, my selfe of truth deprive.

Truth, he contends, is as fine as beauty, and no-one holds a monopoly of such things: and so

> let none despayre
> But to finde as fayre as you.

A slight irregularity in the quatrain of each stanza gives contrast and grace to the metre. The female reply to this move (in the thirteenth poem) is subtle and closely knit. The speaker addresses Love and begs him to take her side:

> Be just, and strike him, too, that dares contemne thee so.

Then, praising his marksmanship:

> No eyes are like to thine, though men suppose thee blinde.

Vengeance obtained, she dreams of a mutual healing of love's wounds 'in some unhaunted shade', but sees that such hopes are vain, and recalls that it is not for her to make such complaints.

Images of wounding and healing recur with obsessive frequency in Campion's later poetry. In poem 14 we have the image of wounding (by beauty) and another medical image—of insanity:

> The first step to madnesse
> Is the excesse of sadnesse.

In poem 15 this theme is considered in a metaphysical light:

> Fairenesse seene in th'outward shape,
> Is but th' inward beauties Ape.

As appearance is subordinate to reality, so is the body to the soul, and the eye to the heart:

> All's but a colour or a shade,
> And neyther alwayes true . . .

> Soule is the Man; for who will so
> The body name?

> Love in the bosome is begot,
> Not in the eyes.

In poem 16 Campion recalls the language of *My sweetest Lesbia*
(R.B. I, 1) in a new access of disappointment:

> Why should I languish, hating light?
> Better to sleepe an endlesse night.

Generalising from his own distress, he expresses a psychiatric
truth:

> 'Tis their best med'cine that are pain'd
> All thought to loose of past delight.

Poem 17, in Campion's favourite verse form, has a lively train
of thought. It opens with a lover's complaint that Nature has
endowed his mistress with so much beauty that 'shee had no
leasure left to make her true'; he then goes on to consider
whether he would prefer to see her less fair, but rejects this idea
and concludes on an unusual note:

> Shee hath more beauty than becomes the chast.

The homely fourteener is brought to life when the woman, in
poem 18, reads her lover a lesson on the art of wooing and teases
him with some compassion:

> Learne to speake first, then to wooe: to wooing, much pertayneth:
> Hee that courts us, wanting Arte, soon falters when he fayneth,
> Lookes a-squint on his discourse, and smiles, when hee complaineth.

The last lines are a nice corrective for the humourless poetry of
disprized love, and a subtle answer to the priggish tone of the
twelfth poem.

> Ruth forgive me, if I err'd, from humane hearts compassion,
> When I laught sometimes too much to see thy foolish fashion:
> But, alas, who lesse could doe that found so good occasion!

The nineteenth poem is one of those to which Campion presumably referred in his preface *To the Reader*: 'if any squeamish
stomackes shall checke at two or three vaine Ditties in the end of
this Booke, let them powre off the clearest and leave those as
dregs in the bottome. Howsoever, if they be but conferred with
the *Canterbury Tales* of that venerable poet Chaucer, they will
then appear toothsome enough.' The salacity is mild and the
poem, which plays with the imagery of flight and pursuit, brings

nothing new or memorable. The same images are more successfully used in poem 20. Whereas in the previous poem the pursuer
complains that he cannot contend with a spirit, in this one the
pursued rejoices in freedom, and also identifies herself with
Love:

> Turne darknesse into day,
> Conjectures into truth,
> Beleeve what th' envious say,
> Let age interpret youth:
>   True love will yet be free,
>   In spite of Jealousie.

A wave of impotence which cost him the favours of a mistress
leads him, in poem 21, to the paradox of loving one who rejects
him because he appeared to be unmoved by her love, and now
'though shee sees, shee'le not believe'.

Poems 22 and 23 are revised versions of earlier poems (R.B. I,
16 and 17). In each case the revisions are beneficial, stale images
being replaced by sharper and sometimes by startling ones. In
poem 22 Campion seems to have discovered Donne's blend of
the euphonious and the discordant: contrast, for example, the
first and second versions of stanza 1:

1st version:

> Mistris, since you so much desire
> To know the place of Cupids fire,
> In your faire shrine that flame doth rest,
> Yet never harbourd in your brest,
> It bides not in your lips so sweete,
> Nor where the rose and lillies meete
> But a little higher, but a little higher;
> There, there, O there lies Cupids fire.

2nd version:

> Beauty, since you so much desire
> To know the place of Cupids fire,
> About you somewhere doth it rest,
> Yet never harbour'd in your brest,
> Nor gout-like in your heele or toe;
> What foole would seeke Loves flame so low?
> But a little higher, but a little higher,
>   There, there, O there lyes Cupids fire.

Again, in poem 23 the tone is different from that of the earlier version, the epigram or general instance replacing the sigh or interjection. In general, a classical, objective mode replaces one which is basically romantic, and a strict metre replaces one with looser texture; e.g.

> Then come, sweetest, come,
>   My lips with kisses gracing;
> Here let us harbour all alone,
>   Die, die in a sweete embracing.
>   (R.B. I, 17)

> O come, while we may,
>   Let's chayne Love with embraces;
> Wee have not all times time to stay,
>   Nor safety in all places.
>   (IV, 23)

The last poem conveys the perplexities of an adolescent in disarmingly simple language. The words sing themselves, and have a haunting quality most appropriate for their position at the end of the book. A medical allusion to a form of anaemia once common in young girls does not disturb the flow:

> Maids are full of longing thoughts that breed a bloudlesse
>   sicknesse,
> And that, oft I heare men say, is onely cur'd by quicknesse.

In sudden desperation she talks of flying 'to some holy Order', but at once recalls her true vocation:

> As I was by one brought forth I would bring forth another.

9

SUPERFLUOUS BLOSSOMS

IN addition to the poetry of his five books of airs and four masques, English poems by Campion appeared in the appendix of a pirated edition of Sidney's *Astrophel and Stella* (1591), in *Observations on the Art of English Poesie* (1601), in *Songs of Mourning* (1613) and in *The Ayres that were sung and played at Brougham Castle* (1618). Individual poems also appeared in Francis Davison's *Poetical Rapsody* (1601) and Richard Alison's *An Howre's Recreation in Musicke* (1606), and there are dedicatory verses in books by Barnabe Barnes (1606), Alphonso Ferrabosco (1609) and Thomas Ravenscroft (1614).

The five *Cantos* of 1591 were signed *Content*. Since the first of them is the same as poem 19 of Rosseter's *Booke of Ayres*, Part I (*Harke, al you ladies*), the set can reasonably be attributed to Campion. This view, Vivian notes, is supported by the close similarity of *Canto quarto* to Epigram 54 in the second book of Epigrams. The diversity of form and continuity of subject in this group of poems link them with Campion's known publications and there are some characteristic felicities. *Canto secundo* reads like the *précis* of a masque: a pageant of glittering ladies is discovered by a band of 'dolorous' knights, their hair 'torne with wrathful hand' and cheeks painted black; suddenly music sounds, and the knights dance with the ladies, and then

> Streight downe under a shadow for wearines they lie
> With pleasant daliance, hand knit with arme in arme,
> Now close, now set aloof . . .

After which they are seen embarking on a pilgrimage 'towards Loves holy land, faire Paphos or Cyprus'. The metre, curiously like Robert Bridges' late alexandrines in texture, reflects the subject of the poem and half conceals one of Campion's favourite rhyme schemes (ababcc)[1]. The theme of pretended evasion,

[1] In his edition of *The Works of Thomas Campion* (see Bibliography), W. R. Davis describes the metre of this poem as 'rimed Asclepiadic, after Sidney's "O sweet woods the delight of solitarines", in *Arcadia*'.

mock kisses and other subtleties of love play are also characteristic.

The third Canto is an epigram, but with the three additional stanzas that follow it in Robert Jones' *Second Booke of Ayres* (1601) it becomes a lyric with a memorable refrain at the end of each stanza. Both metre and idea are strict. His love binds him with a kiss not to stay, but kisses—the seals of love—have an opposite effect; her motives may therefore have been unkind. The fourth Canto, another epigram, is a neat example of Campion's wit and an example of one of his favourite images:

> Love whets the dullest wittes, his plagues be such:
> But makes the wise, by pleasing, doat as much.
> So wit is purchast by this dire disease.
> O let me doat! so Love be bent to please!

(Compare Yeats' 'O what am I, that I should not seem For the song's sake a fool!')

High-spirited youth and moralising age seem to be linked in the fifth Canto. It starts with a complaint over the transitoriness of joy, and continues with a song of expostulations and rhetorical questions:

> What plague is greater than the griefe of mind?
> The griefe of minde that eates in everie vaine,
> In everie vaine that leaves such clods behind,
> Such clods behind as breed such bitter paine,
> So bitter paine that none shall ever finde,
> What plague is greater than the griefe of minde.

The tiresome trick of repeating the end of each line at the beginning of the next is subtly redeemed by the return to the first line of the stanza; and the last stanza breaks away from a leaden echo of Fulke Greville to a golden one that curiously anticipates a well-known song from Dekker's *Patient Grissell* (1603).

Here, for example, are two lines from Campion's poem:

> Doth sorrowe fret thy soule? O direful spirit!
> Doth pleasure feede thy heart? O blessed man!

And these are the opening lines of Dekker's poem:

> Art thou poor, yet hast thou golden slumbers?
> O sweet content!

> Art thou rich, yet is thy mind perplexed?
> O punishment!

Perhaps it is no accident that Dekker's lines are about *Content*, which Campion used as his pen-name.

Another variation on this theme is the poem by Campion that Richard Alison included in his collection of madrigals, *An Howre's Recreation in Musicke* (1606):

> What if a day, or a month, or a yeare
>   Crown thy delights with a thousand sweet contentings?
> Cannot a chance of a night or an howre
>   Crosse thy desires with as many sad tormentings?

Vivian has commented on the great popularity of this song. From the reference to it in Samuel Butler's *Hudibras* (I, 3, 9) it was still familiar in 1663, and it is one of the few poems of Campion which were reprinted (by Chappell in 1838) before the rediscovery of Campion at the end of the nineteenth century. It seems unlikely that the poem without the music would have attracted much attention. Its ideas are, for the most part, trite reflections on the passage of time and the transience of human joy, but one passage has a metaphysical flavour that contrasts tartly with the nostalgic sentiment of the other lines:

> Earthes but a point to the world, and a man
>   Is but a point to the worlds compared centure:
> Shall then the point of a point be so vaine
>   As to triumph in a seelly points adventure?

In 1612 Prince Henry, the elder son of King James, died after an illness (now thought to have been porphyria[1]). The young prince was popular, and his court at St. James' Palace is said to have been more frequented than that of the King, who asked peevishly 'will he bury me alive?' Poets reflected the general feeling in their elegies, which sound a note of exaggerated and and almost hysterical sorrow. Lord Herbert of Cherbury, for example, declared that posterity would grow virtuous only in remembering his virtues:

[1] Ida Macalpine, R. Hunter and C. Rimington, *Porphyria – a royal malady*, British Medical Association, 1968.

> We then are dead, for what doth now remain
> To please us more, or what can we call pain
>   Now we have lost him?

Donne sounded the same note, but with characteristic overtones:

> . . . Therefore wee
> May safelyer say, that we are dead, then hee.
> So, if our griefs wee do not well declare,
> We have double excuse; he is not dead, and we are.

Campion's *Songs of Mourning, bewailing the untimely Death of Prince Henry*, set to music by John Coperario, were published in 1613. The work opens with an elegy in heroic couplets, followed by a series of addresses, each in a different stanza form, to King James, to Queen Anne, to Prince Charles, to Princess Elizabeth, to her husband Frederick V, the Elector Palatine of the Rhine (who is also dedicatee of the book), to Great Britain and to the World. In the elegy Campion adopts a legal framework, calling on the powers of light and darkness to arrest Fate, 'the fellon and the traytour to our state'. He extols the Prince, and finds him a paragon

> Full of coelestiall witchcraft, winning all
> To admiration and love personall.

Though warlike, he was endowed with the arts of peace, which Campion records with a characteristic image.

> When Court and Musicke cal'd him, off fell armes,
> And as hee had been shap't for loves alarmes,
> In harmony hee spake . . .

Having cursed Fate, Campion goes on (surprisingly) to bless 'all-seeing providence' for preserving the King and Prince Charles.

Addressing King James, Campion again uses the image of Fate, contemplating the ravages of grief and death on the human countenance. There is wit as well as poignancy in some of the lines:

> O Fate, why shouldst thou take from Kings their joy and treasure?
>   Their image if men should deface
>   'Twere death, which thou dost race [raze or erase]
>   Even at thy pleasure.

The address to Queen Anne, however, is a more conventional
string of lamentations with some hyperbole:

> Now, Musicke, fill this place
> With thy most dolefull breath:
> O singing wayle a fate more truely funerall
> Than when with all his sonnes the sire of Troy did fall.

Such exaggeration, however, is acceptable as a measure of
feeling, like the cry of Landor's deserted maiden ('But O, who-
ever felt as I?'), and the elegy, as a whole, is restrained, dignified
and well designed for music.

Addressing Prince Charles, Campion seasons the inevitable
but decorous clichés with a pun:

> What gayne can he heape up, though showers of Crownes descend,
> Who for that good must change a brother and a friend?

He then calls on heaven to bless the living Prince with all the
graces of his dead brother. To the Princess Elizabeth, as to
Prince Charles, he speaks of the tragedy of love, that heaven-born
affection, made subject to earthly change.

The next elegy, to Count Frederick, subtly changes the key of
mourning to one of hope and renewal:

> Teares to the dead are due, let none forbid
> Sad harts to sigh; true griefe cannot be hid.

> Yet the most bitter storme to height encreased
>   By heav'n againe is ceased . . .
>   Thoughts with the dayes must change; as tapers waste,
>   So must our griefes; day breakes when night is past.

'To the most disconsolate Great Brittaine' Campion declares
that plague, famine and civil war caused less affliction in her
looks than the loss of their prince; a distasteful observation, but
probably correct. And 'to the World' he utters a curious message
of regret that the warlike prince did not live to set free souls
oppressed under the yoke of infidels.[1]

---

[1] This probably refers to the Prince's militant opposition to the Catholics.
When King James proposed to marry him to a French Catholic he was so
'resolved that two religions should not lie in his bed' that he prepared to
fly to the continent to marry a German Protestant. See G. M. Trevelyan,
England under the Stuarts, London, 1904, p. 117.

Another laureate work with words almost certainly by Campion
is the book of *Ayres that were sung and played at Brougham Castle
in Westmorland* (1618). These ten songs, which were set to music
by George Mason and John Earsden, were written as an entertainment for the King presented by the Earl of Cumberland and
his son, Lord Clifford. The earl was a descendant of that Clifford
(the ninth earl) who fought for Henry VI in the Wars of the Roses,
and was known for his cruelties as 'The Butcher'. The son of the
ninth earl inherited his father's disgrace, and lived for some
years in disguise as a shepherd, but was pardoned and received
back to his father's estates on the accession of Henry VII–an
event which Wordsworth celebrated in his *Song at the Feast of
Brougham Castle.* In Wordsworth's imagined entertainment the
minstrel sings in the romantic heroic tradition about ancestral
glories and the days when victories will come again, but the
shepherd earl is mellowed by his years of contact with Nature,
and abjures 'the savage virtue of the Race'.

Mason and Earsden's entertainment is of a different order.
The first piece, 'a dialogue sung the first night, the King
being at supper', is a eulogy of music, metrically tailored for
music in a manner typical of Campion. There is another reminder
of Campion, Doctor of Physicke, and deviser of masques, in the
grotesque opening:

> Tune thy chearefull voyce to mine;
>   Musicke helpes digesting,
> Musicke is as good as wine,
>   And as fit for feasting.

The second poem, also a dialogue at dinner, praises the king, but
might have found its place in the *Divine and Morall Songs.* In
The Kings Good-night a similar fulsomeness is relieved by the
touch of wit and music, especially in the figure of James as a sun
rising in the North:

> The Northerne morne is best,
> And so, best King, good rest.

There is more poetry and a reminder of the world of Puck and
Oberon in the fourth song, addressed to those

> Friends of night, that oft have done
> Homage to the horned Moone.

In the fifth poem the scene is again abruptly changed. A divine right of kings to disregard the conventions of sexual love is the moral drawn, with possibly unconscious irony, from the story of Dido and Aeneas:

> Dido wept, but what of this?
>   The Gods would have it so:
> Aeneas nothing did amisse,
>   For hee was forc't to goe.
> Learne, Lordings, then, no faith to keepe
> With your Loves, but let them weepe:
>   'Tis folly to be true:
> Let this Story serve your turne,
> And let twenty Didoes burne
>   So you get daily new.

The poem that follows is for dancing, and conveys the mood with simplicity of images and rhythms reminiscent of Jack and Joan in the *First Booke of Ayres*. And then:

> The shadowes darkning our intents
> Must fade, and Truth now take her place.

So begins the seventh song, in the sequel to which the 'truth' is predicted–a conventional inventory of long life, enduring power, endless posterity, peace, love and honour, ending with adulation fit for a Roman emperor:

> So humbly prostrate at thy sacred feete
> Our nightly sports and prophesies wee end.

Nevertheless there are two more songs–possibly an after-thought, but artistically finer than the 'prophesies', and not unlike some poems of the later song-books in their musical and epigrammatic style. The ninth song complains that 'blest houres soone consume, But joylesse pass at Leasure', while the tenth returns to the theme of love and the image of Jupiter which is half implicit in the *Ballad* on Dido and Aeneas:

> Princely Guests, wee wish there were
> Joves Nectar and Ambrosia here
>   That you might like immortals feed,
> Changing shapes like full-fed Jove
> In the sweet pursuit of love.

10

MUSIC OF THE LATER SONG-BOOKS

The settings in the four books of airs are not uniform in quality, but a selection of the best songs gives us an idea of the varied delights of Campion's music. The songs are strophic, frequently with repetition of the last two lines of each verse. A notable exception is *Faine would I wed* (IV, 24), a special case which will be discussed later on.

Campion is primarily a writer of melodies; in his songs the accompaniment is always a support for the voice part, whereas with Dowland, for instance, the more polyphonic style results in the voice part's fusing into the texture of the part-writing. The chordal style of the accompaniment is simple; it follows the voice with little rhythmic life of its own. There is a rare instance of independence at the opening of *Oft have I sigh'd* (III, 1) and the introductory bar of *Thus I resolve* (III, 22). The texture of the music shows a strong polarity between the voice (top) part and the bass. This is generally considered a distinguishing feature of the Baroque era, but it belongs as much to the English lutenist song writers as to the much-publicised Italian monodists. Between the bass and top parts the harmony is improvisatory in character, and lute technique is often evident in the disappearance of a part for a few beats, in consecutive fifths and octaves, and in bass leaps of a seventh up from the gamut G.

The concept of the major and minor key system had not crystallised in Campion's time, and harmony was thus in a state of flux, untrammelled by conventions; much music of the time has to our ears a refreshing freedom by suggesting passage through keys without using more than simple chords mostly in root position. At the opening of *Out of my soules deapth to thee* (I, 4) there is a tortuous sequence of triads which serve to underline the first words of the first verse—G major, C, A, D, G minor and D. In *Come, chearfull day* (I, 17) at the last two lines of each verse there is a sudden move from G major to B flat. After a modulation to the relative minor, G minor, a tierce de Picardie serves to bring the music back to G major.

A more subtle juxtaposition of common chords is found in *To Musicke bent* (I, 7). The melody by itself suggests little of the harmony. In the first phrase, which starts in C minor, the appearance of the E flat and F major chords gives a dreamlike quality.

In the fifth bar, the secure B natural of the G major chord, giving an orthodox progression in C minor, is undermined by the strange B flat in the lute part, luring the voice to it.

We can never be sure that harmony which is peculiarly satisfying to our ears had the same effect when it was written nearly four hundred years ago: we listen conditioned by the music of the intervening years. This example is from *Young and simple though I am* (IV, 9).

The melody is led to the chord of C by the F natural in the lute part. Since the chord of G could well have been retained, this

produces a pleasing conflict, and involves a rich chord on the
second quaver (suggesting, in modern terms, a dominant ninth).
The justification for picking out such examples lies in their
context. Thus in heavily chromatic music, chords of the seventh
and ninth proliferate and pass unnoticed, whilst when they
occur in a much simpler style they are to be savoured. It is
reasonable to think that they sounded thus to Campion's
contemporaries.

Examples of remarkable harmony are often points of outstanding word-painting, such as is found in *Oft have I sigh'd*
(III, 1. b. 18–24). Campion repeats twice the words 'yet I languish
still', wringing out their melancholy with the tension of a suspended note and a strange progression of chords.

Discords, where they occur, are a result of prepared suspensions and the false relations which are a feature of late sixteenth-
century music. Within this framework Campion on occasion
achieves great poignancy. This instance is from *Author of light*
(I, 1), one of the best songs. The chord of the seventh over the
E flat yields yet another discord as the D moves on to C and the
B flat in the voice part moves on to A, giving an effect of exceeding richness. The agony of the words could not have been better
served.

One of the most involved instances of suspension occurs in
Leave prolonging thy distresse (IV, 1.): the first C in the lute part,
instead of waiting for the voice's B flat to resolve on to the A,
moves to a discordant B flat, resulting in parallel sevenths.

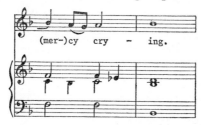

Discords resulting from independent movement of parts are
common in late Renaissance music. Each part sung by itself has
smoothness and sense of direction: this is what makes the resulting discords so fascinating to the ear.

Suspensions in sequence, so common a device that they can
often sound hackneyed, are used discreetly by Campion. They
are employed descending in *Fire, fire* (III, 20) to the words 'O
drowne both mee' (in the first verse at least), and ascending in
a graceful phrase in *Her rosie cheekes* (II, 20). At the final
cadence of this song there is a discord formed by the key-note G
being anticipated in the voice against the leading-note F sharp
on the lute–the opposite of a suspension.

L

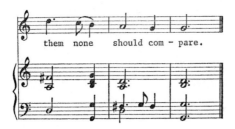

them none   should com – pare.

Such discords became common in the music of the English Restoration composers.

In *Sweet, exclude mee not* (II, 11), the sequential suspensions are particularly effective; in addition to the chords of the seventh produced by the suspended note, the E flat following the D minor chord,–also the shape of the melody, because it is independent of the accompaniment,–make this passage fine.

From him   that ere long must bed   thee:

A further source of delight is the twist given to the harmony by false relations (the successive sounding of a note and its flattened or sharpened form) disrupting our sense of major and minor. The finest example is in the third bar of *Now let her change* (III, 2). At this point in each verse the weird feeling produced by the C major-minor clash and the consecutive fifths in the bass subtly interpret the meaning of the words: 'she proves strange', 'vexe her with unkindnesse', 'Once false proves faithful never'. The opening four bars are quoted partly because they are necessary for the full effect of bar 3, and also because they show the duality between G minor and major which reflects nicely the deceit complained of in the poem (although this effect may be a result rather of the conventional use of the tierce de Picardie than of the composer's design–the final chord of every cadence throughout the four books is either major or without a third). The melody is strong and the firmness of the first phrase well answered by the second; the attraction in the rhythm lies at the end of each phrase with its long repeated notes.

This is one of the many Campion poems that were set by other composers. Pilkington's version is similar to Campion's in several ways.

The melodic form of the songs shows considerable variety, particularly in phrase structure. Let us consider three examples of this variety.

Many of the songs are in binary form. Sometimes the first, sometimes the second, and sometimes both halves are repeated. This is essentially a musical consideration and often involves repetition of words at the repeat of the second half. *To Musicke bent* (I, 7) is binary, with both halves of the melody repeated. In *Most sweet and pleasing* (I, 9) and *Wise men patience never want* (I, 10) the first half is repeated but not the second, and in *Tune thy Musicke to thy hart* (I, 8) the second is repeated and not the first. Repeating the words as well as the music in the second half effectively echoes the last lines of each verse.

Some of the through-composed melodies show evidence of having grown from one idea. (A through-composed melody is one without phrase repetition of the kind found in binary form.) In

Her rosie cheekes (II, 20) the rising scale with a falling note at the end of it with which the song commences is the basis of the next extended phrase and later is inverted.

Another through-composed song springing from one idea is *Think'st thou to seduce me then* (IV, 18).

    Faine would I wed (IV, 24) is unique in its form. The same accompaniment is used for each of the three verses but the melody changes, so that the song is in the form of three divisions over a ground. The chord sequence is reminiscent of the passamezzo, the dance form of the sixteenth century.

breed   a   bloud - lesse   sicke - nesse,
one - ly   cur'd   by   quick - nesse.

The complete melody covering the three verses is found with
slight variations in a keyboard piece of Richard Farnaby (Giles'
son) in the Fitzwilliam Virginal Book—the main difference being
that Campion has repeated each phrase, presumably to make it
fit the words. In the *Musica Britannica* edition of Farnaby's
works the dates of the copying of the Fitzwilliam Virginal Book
are given as between 1609 and 1619. Fellowes suggests 1617 as
the publication date of Campion's fourth book of airs, so there
seems little way of telling which version came first. The tune is
very like a folk-song and may have been known as such to both
composers. It is, as David Greer points out, almost identical
with a popular tune of the seventeenth century called *Goddesses*
or *Quodling's Delight*, and is varied in successive stanzas in a
manner that suggests the tradition of improvisation.[1]
    The simplest melodies have a regularity of phrase length
(usually 2 or 4 bars) and some are hymn-like in nature—indeed
some are sung as hymns (for example, *Never weather-beaten
Saile* (I, 11) and *Sing a Song of joy* (I, 15) are both to be found in
Songs of Praise). *Wise men patience never want* (I, 10) has the
character of a pleasant, eminently singable hymn. The tune
consists of six two-bar phrases of identical rhythm except for
two passing-notes in one phrase. This similarity occurs also in
the two-bar phrases of *View mee, Lord, a Worke of Thine* (I, 5).
The man of life upright (I, 2), *To Musicke bent* (I, 7) and *Most
sweet and pleasing* (I, 9) all have this regularity throughout.
These songs are all from Book 1, but examples are found
throughout the four books: *The peacefull westerne winde* (II, 12),
Be thou then my beauty (III, 19) and *Ev'ry Dame affects good fame*
(IV, 5). Such melodies, as may be expected, are not among

[1] 'Campion the Musician', *Lute Society Journal*, 1967, **9**, p. 7.

Campion's most interesting, unless they are distinguished by other factors. The harmonic subtlety of *To Musicke bent* (I, 7) has already been noted (p. 151). *The peacefull westerne winde* and *Be thou then my beauty* are particularly beautiful tunes with a smooth rhythm and a shape reminiscent of folk-song.

There are frequent examples of melodies constructed in phrases of three regular stresses. *Respect my faith* (IV, 2), *To Musicke bent* (I, 7) and *Most sweet and pleasing* (I, 9) are of this kind, and furthermore have an almost identical rhythmic pattern. Some of the most interesting melodies derive their quality from the asymmetry of their phrases. *Love me or not* (IV, 10) and *Tune thy Musicke to thy hart* (I, 8) both consist of five-bar phrases (although in the original edition the phrases of five stresses in *Love me or not* are barred irregularly); each phrase subdivides into a two-bar followed by a three-bar phrase. The first five bars of *Tune thy Musicke to thy hart* are distinguished by a particularly beautiful cadence, which owes its effect to the delaying of the tonic chord (E flat at this point) and the return of the melody up to B flat (the fifth of the chord) at the end.

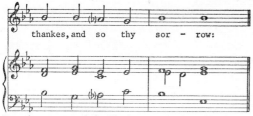

thankes, and   so   thy   sor - row:

In the second half the melody climbs upwards by semitones, involving the harmony in a chromatic passage; this occurs fairly frequently elsewhere in the songs. In this example the words are not descriptive; but the chromatic rising at the end of *Author of light* (I, 1) is an instance of highly expressive word-painting, in both verses. The descending bass line in contrary motion with the rising semitones of the melody makes this a particularly striking passage.

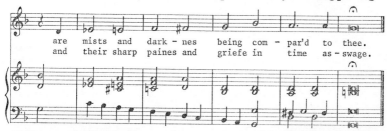

are   mists and   dark - nes   being com - par'd to thee.
and   their sharp paines and   griefe in time as - swage.

Many melodies built on phrases repeated in rhythm or shape alter in phrase-length towards the end. *Pin'd I am and like to die* (II, 14) consists in its first half of a phrase of five and a half bars repeated, and in its second, a four-bar phrase (if we adapt the bar-lines to reflect the stresses) which is repeated. The attraction lies in the squareness of the second half contrasted with the first. *Never weather-beaten Saile* (I, 11), perhaps the best-known song due to its popularity as a hymn, is constructed in four-bar phrases, the last of which is extended to six bars by a sequential repetition of one bar. The words 'O come quickly' are also repeated; the disruption in the flow of melody underlines the urgent plea of the poem.

O come quick-ly,   O   come quick-ly,   O   come quick-ly,
sweet-est Lord, and   take my soule to   rest.

Campion's use of sequence often has the pleasing effect of hastening the rate of movement by shortening the phrase lengths. It happens in *Shall I come, sweet Love, to thee?* (III, 17). The first half consists of four-bar phrases with leisurely extended final notes; the second half is a much shorter descending phrase which repeats in breathless sequence until it finds the keynote at the end of its descent: 'Let me not, for pitty, more, Tell the long houres at your dore':

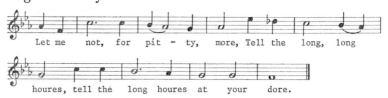

Usually he employs the device of sequence in the service of the words; in his hands it also contributes to the overall shape of the melody. *Beauty since you so much desire* (IV, 22) is one of the through-composed melodies. The words in both verses lead to the conclusion that Cupid's fire lies a little higher than in heel or toe. They are matched by a fine musical climax built in a sequence, to the words 'but a little higher', and a lengthening of notes with the reply 'There, O there lyes Cupids fire' (b. 13-end):

A similar rising sequence followed by a broad passage in longer notes is found in *Sweet, exclude mee not* (II, 11). The words entice the hesitant girl through the sequence and finally proclaim the answer to all doubts:

> Presume then yet a little more:
> Here's the way, barre not the dore.

The subject of the words is the same in both instances.

In *Oft have I sigh'd* (III, 1) a sequence occurs at the beginning.

After four introductory chords on the lute, these first four words are sung three times, twice in languishing minims; the third time the singer braces herself to continue the account of her woes by shortening the notes to crotchets:

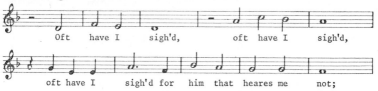

The word-painting in the second half of this song has already been mentioned.

Undoubtedly the variety of phrase structure is one of the most attractive features of Campion's style. The melodies range from the straightforward, square construction of *Wise men patience never want* (I, 10), through the five-bar phrases of *Tune thy Musicke to thy hart* (I, 8), and the differing phrase-lengths of first and second half in *Pin'd I am and like to die* (II, 14) to the fluid phrases of melodies where the juxtaposition of duple, triple and quadruple metres gives the melodic line a spring at each unexpected stress. An example of this is found in *Vaine men whose follies* (II, 1), which is quoted complete on p. 167.

Give beauty all her right (II, 7) also has this 'sprung rhythm'. It is particularly delightful when our predictions on the course of a sequence are confounded as at the end of this song.

Her rosie cheekes (II, 20) has already been mentioned as a song with a melody that grows from its opening idea (pp. 155–6). This feeling of growth is enhanced by the first three phrases which are two, three and four bars long respectively. The second half of the melody maintains this irregularity with metres alternating between two and three.

In *There is a Garden in her face* (IV, 7) the looseness of rhythm in the random repetitions of 'Cherry ripe' suggests the street cry. As with other features of Campion's music, some instances of

rhythmic irregularity seem to have been determined by the
words and others by purely musical considerations. The irregular
metres of *Think'st thou to seduce me then?* (IV, 18), for example,
seem to have been dictated rather by musical whim than by
attention to words.

The simplest tunes employ stepwise movement, leaps covering
concordant intervals and very few chromatic notes (*The man of
life upright* (I, 2), *Wise men patience never want* (I, 10), *Never
weather-beaten Saile* (I, 11), and *The peacefull westerne winde*
(II, 12) are four examples.) Such tunes for the most part suggest
their harmony and make sense if sung unaccompanied. At the
opposite extreme are the melodies which contain involved chromatic moves and depend on their harmony to make their direction clear. This phrase from *Leave prolonging thy distresse* (IV, 1)
is quite awkward to sing unaccompanied:

And the opening of *Loe, when backe mine eye* (I, 13) makes
nonsense by itself (bars 1–3):

The same chromatic alteration of a note at close proximity is
found in *The man of life upright* (I, 2)

and in *So tyr'd are all my thoughts* (III, 5). The chromaticism,
unlike that of the rising passages in *Author of light* (I, 1) (quoted
above) and in *Tune thy Musicke to thy hart* (I, 8), appears arbi-
trary; often the purpose of such awkward turns is to achieve a
tierce de Picardie at any price.

Several fine songs are of a type which may be called 'declamatory'. The characteristics are an initial chord in the accompaniment before the voice enters, and the rhythmically fluid vocal
phrases interspersed with rests, which follow carefully the word-
quantities—a recitative-like style. There is also generally an
absence of exact repetition, so frequent in the other songs. The
already much-quoted *Author of light* provides an outstanding

example. Its first phrase has the same shape in rhythm and interval as that of *Kinde are her answeres* (III, 7) which is similar in style to *Author of light*, but constructed in more regular phrases. There is a delicate balance of rhythm and shape in the phrase 'O, did ever voice so sweet but only fain?'

O griefe, O spight (III, 8) and *O sweet delight* (III, 21) are further examples; perhaps there is a connection between this declamatory style and the vocative openings of many of the poems so set. *Come chearfull day* (I, 17), another declamatory song like *Oft have I sigh'd* (III, 1), commences with a rising sequence which increases in speed on repetition. This is balanced by a decrease in speed at the end of the song after a descending sequence to the words 'So ev'ry day we live, a day wee dye'. This song has already been mentioned in connection with the unique change of key at the beginning of the second section, from G to B flat. *Breake now my heart* (III, 10) opens with a feeling of languor, created by the stillness of the lute part and the drooping vocal phrases; in style

and pathos it is comparable with Monteverdi recitative. (The lute part in the original edition is printed a fourth higher than the voice part: it would probably have been performed in C minor, giving a gamut G in bar 5 instead of the low D which is outside the range of the lute, with the singer reading his part in the 'easier' key of G minor.)

Some melodies contain memorable phrases which incorporate modal scale passages. At the end of *Pin'd I am* (II, 14) there is a phrase constructed of an ascending and descending scale in the Mixolydian mode—the 'major' scale with flattened seventh:

In a texture where the major and minor modes predominate such a deviation has a welcome freshness. *If any hath the heart to kill* (IV, 21) is almost entirely in the Dorian mode, particularly emphasised by the scale passage which forms the first phrase. The first stanza of *Faine would I wed* (IV, 24) includes versions of scales in the tonality of G minor with seventh and sixth degrees sharpened descending and flattened ascending (see example on p. 156).

Broad, angular lines are also found in the songs, as in *Where are all thy beauties now?* (I, 3), and in *Shall I come, sweet Love, to thee?* (III, 17):

To restore perspective, here are quoted three songs in their entirety. They are among the best, and demonstrate in their diversity the range of Campion's technique. All three have been referred to above, so the commentaries here are brief.

Author of light (I, 1)

The vocal line in this song is interwoven with the lute part more closely than is usual with Campion, creating a polyphonic texture. This results in a song of great intensity, incorporating such masterly touches as the groping of the extended phrase at 'for blinde with worldly vaine desires'. The syncopation in the vocal line at this point and also in bars 23–28 is particularly effective. The harmony in bars 3–5 and 28–33 has already been commented upon. (The key of course is G minor, although the signature is B flat.)

blinde with world-ly vaine ___ de - sires, I wan-der as a stray.
faint and fad - ing hart ___ can raise, and in joyes bo - some place.

Sunne and Moone, Starres and un - der lights I see, But all ___ their glo - rious beames are mists and dark - nes, being com - par'd to thee.

Sinne and Death, Hell and tempt - ing Fiends may rage; But God ___ his owne ___ will guard, and their sharp paines and griefe in time as - swage.

Vaine men whose follies (II, 1)

This song has a lively rhythm which seems to keep changing step; this, together with the graceful rise and fall of the melody, makes it highly satisfying. The poem is about the fickle nature of love. The quicker notes and sharp rhythms of the second half

2. How faire an entrance breakes the way to love!
   How rich of golden hope and gay delight!
   What hart cannot a modest beauty move?
   Who, seeing cleare day once, will dreame of night?
   Shee seem'd a Saint, that brake her faith with mee,
   But prov'd a woman as all other be.

3. So bitter is their sweet, that true content
   Unhappy men in them may never finde.
   Ah, but without them none; both must consent,
   Else uncouth are the joys of eyther kinde.
   Let us then prayse their good, forget their ill;
   Men must be men, and women women still.

convey the unsentimental philosophic flavour of the words. (In the original edition each bar contains two minims' worth of notes; to the modern reader this obscures the rhythm so effectively that the barring in this example has been modernised, and the time-signature consequently omitted.)

Oft have I sigh'd (III, 1)

The despair in the words is reflected in the hesitancy with which the song commences. Bars 18–23 are outstanding in their

Who ab - sent hath both love and mee for - got.
His faith-lesse stay some kind-nesse would ex - cuse:

O —— yet I lan-guish still, yet I lan-guish.
O —— yet I lan-guish still, yet I lan-guish

still, yet I lan-guish still through his de -
still, yet I lan-guish still still con-stant

lay: Dayes seeme as yeares when
mourne For him that can breake

wisht friends breake their day.
vowes but not re - turne.

M

portrayal of the loneliness of desertion, through the progression of strangely disconnected chords.

Our speculations on Campion as an artist are the more fascinating since we have at our disposal two facets of his abilities linked together in his songs. To represent him convincingly it is necessary to separate these elements. The nature of lute-song literature is intimate, the gestures are subtle. Once we are attuned to their dimensions, we can see the extent of Campion's range. There is pious and unaffected simplicity in his religious songs; in the love songs there is sometimes pathos and sometimes an ingenuous quality which, when considered with the words, emerges as a finely judged understatement; and in the more introspective songs there is the most telling expression of mental anguish.

I I

MUSICAL THEORY

WORKS of musical theory derive their interest mainly from their relation to the music being written in their time. Since they are mostly intended for teaching purposes, they cannot represent the *avant garde* of their age; time has to elapse before the essence of a style becomes clear enough to be set down as a guide. And what do they teach? There have been different claims at different times. The least ambiguous, and the most common in sixteenth-century treatises, is the claim to teach composition. But there has always lurked the feeling that composition cannot be taught; the assumption is that it is a naturally endowed gift. This view has been held to a lesser or greater extent at different times. The nineteenth century was the period of the genius, when the composer was a man apart; with this went the feeling that the ability to compose was a gift from heaven. This process and its product were not to be sullied by contact with the more mundane activities of life. In this atmosphere, the unteachable nature of composition would be stressed. Musical theory would be confined to teaching harmony and counterpoint with the imitation of older styles (Palestrina and Bach) as a measure of competence. In the sixteenth and also in the twentieth century there is less emphasis on the idea of composition as a natural gift; music is seen as a craft, which plays a part in everyday life and whose elements can be taught.

In this spirit were written the greatest English treatise of the sixteenth century, Thomas Morley's *A Plaine and Easie Introduction to Practicall Musicke* (1597), and also Thomas Campion's *A New Way of Making Fowre Parts in Counter-point*. The titles reveal the attitude of a craftsman rather than that of a genius invested with a mysterious gift.

Since composition was regarded as a craft, the idea of originality in music, the 'personal utterance', would have had little meaning. It is therefore not so odd to find composers writing treatises on 'composition' in which is propounded the dead letter

171

of a style with no account taken of the spirit that enlivens composition.

In the dedication (to *The Flowre of Princes, Charles*) Campion mentions the conventional origins of music (invented by Apollo, practised by David the prophet) and, observing his own dual rôle of physician and musician, offers the example of Galen, who, 'the first of Physitions, became so expert a Musition, that he could not containe himselfe, but needes he must apply all the proportions of Musicke to the uncertaine motions of the pulse'. Campion, being more reasonable, contents himself 'with a poore and easie invention; yet new and certaine; by which the skill of Musicke shall be redeemed from much darknesse, wherein envious antiquitie of purpose did involve it'. The gist of Campion's theorising led towards the acceptance of chords as entities at the same time as a polarity between melody and accompaniment was establishing itself. In view of this, the darkness referred to could be connected with the complexity and confusion over words in Renaissance polyphony to which the Italian Camerata objected. Their new style lay in a similar direction to Campion's.

In the Preface Campion commences with a discussion of the ambiguity of musical terms which is unfortunately no less applicable today. In particular he mentions the various meanings of 'tone' and 'note'. He continues with a criticism of the hexachord system as a method of teaching, saying that it was suitable when the total compass of notes was twenty, 'but the liberty of the latter age hath given Musicke more space both above and below, altering thereby the former naming of the Notes'. By the end of the sixteenth century the grouping of notes by octaves had more relevance than the hexachord system of the middle ages which consisted of three sets of six diatonic notes, giving three hexachords starting on C, F and G.

The main body of the treatise is divided into three sections. The first is entitled 'Of Counterpoint'. The fundamental point in Campion's teaching is that the bass is the most important part. 'The parts of Musicke are in all but foure, howsoever some skilfull Musitions have composed songs of twenty, thirty and forty parts:[1] for be the parts never so many, they are but one of these foure in nature. . . . The *Base* which is the lowest part and foundation of the whole song: the *Tenor*, placed next above the

---

[1] This is probably a reference to Tallis's 'Spem in alium'.

Base: next above the *Tenor* the *Meane* or *Counter-Tenor*, and in the highest place the *Treble*.' These four are likened to the elements: bass, to the earth, 'a foundation to the rest. The Tenor is likened to the water, the Meane to the Aire, and the Treble to the Fire. . . . They have also in their native property every one place above the other, the lighter uppermost, the waightiest at the bottome.' With delightful presumption Campion concludes his fanciful nonsense as if he had proceeded according to scientific method: 'Having now demonstrated that there are in all but foure parts, and that the Base is the foundation of the other three, I assume that the true sight and judgement of the upper three must proceed from the lowest.'

His most valid reason for the priority of the bass is that it 'containes in it both the Aire and true judgement of the Key'. The latter point is clear to us; we are used to looking to the bass at cadences to determine the key. But that the bass should determine the treble is clear only from his next point. This is a rule about progression of intervals formed between the bass and any one of the upper parts. 'If the Base shall ascend either a second, third or fourth, that part which stands in the third or tenth above the Base, shall fall into an eight, that which is a fift shall passe into a third, and that which is an eight shall remove into a fift.' This is reduced to a table of figures:

$$8 \qquad 3 \qquad 5$$
$$3 \qquad 5 \qquad 8$$

When the bass descends, the opposite progression takes place; an eighth becomes a third, and so on. Obviously once the bass line and the layout of the first chord are established, there is no option over the notes in the other parts. Campion was proud of this system: 'If I should discover no more then this already deciphered of Counter-point, wherein the native order of foure parts with use of the Concords, is demonstratively expressed, might I be mine own Judge, I had effected more in Counter-point, then any man before me hath ever attempted.' However, the same information in more detail had been given earlier in Morley's *Plaine and Easie Introduction*, Part Three, 'Treating of Composing or Setting of Songs', so Campion is not quite justified in his claim.

It will be seen that a 'vertical' view of music was crystallising;

what became known as a common chord was perceived as an entity rather than as the incidental result of movement of polyphonic parts. In these early stages every possible movement in two-, three- and four-part harmony was charted in theoretical works. The 'rules' of harmony listed what was admissible. When the concept of chords became clearer through use, the 'rules' of harmony were restricted to listing what was inadmissible–consecutive fifths and octaves and so on.

To cover all the possibilities of part progression, Campion has to extend his rule thus: 'That you may perceive how cunning and how certaine nature is in all her operations, know that what Cords have held good in this ascending and descending of the Base answere in the contrary by the very same rule.' This reduces the value of the table (see above). According to Campion's first rule, progression of intervals formed with the bass when it *ascended* could be determined from the table by reading *upwards* from the lower figure to the higher; for a *descending* bass one read *downwards*. Now he amends this by stating that sometimes progression of intervals formed with the bass when it *ascended* would be those represented on the table by reading *downwards*. In other words, the ascent or descent of the bass does not govern progression of intervals.

Passing-notes are introduced as notes which 'break' an interval; thus their inessential character is realised.

Intervals of a sixth are admitted as variants of the fifth, to be followed by the same interval (a third if the bass rises; see table). 'If the Base shall use a sharpe, as in F sharpe, then must we take the sixt of necessity, but the eight to the Base may not be used, so that exception is to be taken against our rule of Counter-point.' Campion's hesitation over doubling F sharp became defined in later centuries as the 'rule' about the inadvisability of doubling the third of a major triad. In 1600 an F sharp would rarely be other than what today we know as the third of the triad of D major. He gives his own reason for not using 'an eight to the Base' where it is F sharp: 'Such Bases are not true Bases, for where a sixt is to be taken, either in F sharpe, or in E sharpe, [i.e. E], or in B or in A the true Base is a third lower–F sharpe in D, E in C, B in G, A in F.' There is here the realisation that a chord consisting for example of F sharp (bass), A and D is but another version of the chord D–F sharp–A. It is the concept of

a triad and its inversions, but it was not until the time of Rameau
that it was so expressed. In his *Traité de l'Harmonie* (1722) chords
are treated as 'absolute and independent entities, detachable
from all content, devoid of any melodic implications and suscep-
tible of scientific analysis and classification'.[1]

Rule is given for the avoidance of the augmented second
(criticised as 'unformall'). Above a stationary bass the parts may
'remove at their pleasure'. Passing notes in the bass do not affect
the progression of parts. In a minor key the note which sub-
sequently became called the leading note must be sharp. Treatment of concordant intervals is concluded by discussion of
sixths (dismissed as 'very imperfect, being compounded of a
third which is an imperfect Concord, and of a fourth which is
a Discord') and of consecutive thirds, one of which must be
'irregular' since such a progression is not covered by the table.
The chapter ends with a direction for the use of the suspended
leading note at a perfect cadence. Campion implies that such a
suspension is obligatory: 'The part must hold, that in holding
can use the fourth or eleaventh [i.e. result in a fourth or an
eleventh with the bass] and so passe eyther into the third or
tenth.'

A remark in the final paragraph following a musical example
reminds us that Campion was a composer: 'In this Aire the last
Note onely is, for sweetnesse sake, altered from the rule. . . .'

The second chapter, 'Of the Tones of Musicke', is a discussion
of tonality—the sense of what key a piece is in, and the methods
of establishing this. Again, the ambiguity in terms is stressed:
'Most necessary . . . for him [a musician] is the true knowledge
of the Key or Moode, or Tone, for all signifie the same thing,
with the closes belonging unto it, for there is no tune that can
have any grace or sweetnesse, unlesse it be bounded within a
proper key, without running into strange keyes which have no
affinity with the aire of the song.' And again Campion is visited

---

[1] *Philosophy of Music Histories*, Dwight Allen, Dover Edn., 1962, p. 64.

by a sense of pioneering, claiming 'in an easie and briefe discourse to endeavour to expresse that, which many in large and obscure volumes have made fearefull to the idle Reader'. (Is this perhaps an oblique reference to Morley's *Plaine and Easie Introduction?*)

He divides the octave into a perfect fifth and fourth, and states that the fifth 'discovers the key, and all the closes pertaining properly thereunto.' The fifth in turn divides into a combination of 'greater' and 'lesser' (major and minor) thirds. Relics of the modal system remain. He describes 'modus authentus' and 'modus plagalii'. An authentic mode begins on its 'centre note' (there were six modes, beginning on D, E, F, G, A and C) and the plagal version begins a fourth lower. The mode that became the basis of a major key was that starting on C; the centre note and the fourth below became the tonic and dominant.

The possible closes for major and minor keys are listed. Effectively, in a minor key, cadences in tonic, dominant and mediant (the relative major) keys are possible. 'The first close is that which maintaines the aire of the key, and may be used often, the second is next to be preferd, and the last, last.' In a major key, tonic, dominant, supertonic and subdominant are possible keys. Campion stresses the importance of key and censures a tune 'ordinarily used, or rather abused, in our Churches, which is begun in one key and ended in another, quite contrary to nature'. He rectifies it 'according to former Rule of Counterpoint'.

At the beginning of the last chapter, 'Of the taking of all Concords, perfect and imperfect', Campion acknowledges a debt to Sethus Calvisius, 'a Germane'. Calvisius was a cantor at the Thomasschule in Leipzig (the post held by J. S. Bach from 1723) and author of several important works on musical theory. He is of interest in relation to Campion because in his writing he was aware of the modern trend towards monody. Hugo Riemann considers Calvisius to be one of those who steered musical studies away from counterpoint and towards harmony.

The rules now given by Campion are most like those to be found in a nineteenth- and twentieth-century theory book, and they would seem to be superfluous if the dicta of the first chapter are followed concerning progression of parts above the bass: for instance, consecutive fifths and octaves are not allowed; a fifth may proceed to an octave, and vice versa, providing one of the parts moves by step.

False relations are condemned. An E, for instance, in one of two parts, followed in the next chord by an E flat in the other part 'begets a false second, which is a harsh discorde, and though these Notes sound not both together, yet in few parts they leave an offence in the eare'.

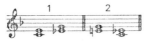

An augmented fourth, 'begotten' in the same manner between adjacent chords, also constitutes an offence. Perhaps the proviso 'in few parts' is important, for in Campion's music false relations figure prominently, particularly for word-painting.

Rules for progressing from minor and major thirds and sixths are given. 'Crossing parts' where both parts move in similar motion, in modern terminology, is disallowed:

By seeking to state all that is allowed, the section is repetitive. The progression of thirds to octaves or fifths for instance can be summed up by prohibiting leaps to octaves and fifths when both parts move in similar motion, whereas Campion finds it necessary to give thirty-two musical examples. He forbids a minor third to become a fifth when the upper part remains on the same note, claiming that in all such cases a major third would be better. He criticises it as yielding 'a most unpleasing harmony' and gives a lengthy musical example to demonstrate; but the unpleasantness is not apparent within the context.

The minor sixth 'regularly goes into the fift, one of the parts holding his place', but there is a strange inconsistency about when it is allowed to pass into an octave: e.g. it is acceptable if the upper part ascends F–B flat and the lower A–B flat, but if the upper part progresses D–G and the lower F sharp–G, it is 'not tollerable'. The only reason given is that 'the Base be sharpe in F fa-ut'. Consecutive minor sixths with their chromaticism are forbidden, 'by reason of the falling in of the Relation not harmonicall'. Major sixths proceed to octaves; to fifths, only when these arise from a progression of sixths being interrupted by suspension in one part.

The treatise ends with another concession. These rules, Campion says, have been given for writing in few parts. Even with few parts to deal with 'for fuge [imitation] and formality sake, some dispensation may be graunted'. But if we write in many parts, necessity may force us to break the rules. However, 'it may the more easily be excused, because the multitude of parts will drowne any small inconvenience'.

INTERACTIONS

A CREATIVE artist's reputation is moulded and gradually stabilised by accretions and weatherings of time. The influence of these forces on Campion's reputation was unusual. Thrust into complete obscurity after his death, the poet emerged as a newcomer to critical attention with Hardy and Yeats, and the composer emerged still later when Hindemith and Walton were newcomers. Nevertheless, he was accepted promptly, not as a novice, but as an elder, and has survived the turbulent changes of twentieth-century taste. An unknown contemporary of Shakespeare would, of course, arrive with some advantages; but the continuing popularity of Campion's work is clearly due to features which give it value and importance to men with widely varying artistic ideals. To the Victorian discoverers of Campion, a mellifluous word-music and an apt expression of sentiment were the special attraction of his verse; today probably more attention is paid to its artistic variety of structure, its relation to musical setting, its epigrammatic precision, and to a shrewdness and sophistication underlying a formal naïvety.

It is tempting to look for mutual influence and interaction of his various activities, and especially of poetry, music and medicine, which he cultivated, as it were, in emulation of Apollo:

> Tres novit, Labiene, Phoebus artes;
> Ut narrant veteres sophi; peraeque
> Quas omnes colui, colamque semper.
> (*Epigrams*, I, 167)

The most obvious of such influences is that of the requirements for musical setting on the form, and especially the metre, of his poems. It is, in a sense, ironic that some of the most individual features of these poems were determined by considerations that had nothing to do with the poetry, as in such lines as these:

> Love me or not, love her I must or dye;
> Leave me or not, follow her needs must I.

or   Kinde are her answeres,
                       But her performance keeps no day;
                   Breaks time, as dancers
                       From their own Musicke when they stray.

The restrictions imposed on the poet by musical setting, like
those imposed by metrical forms such as the sonnet or *terza
rima*, are not obstructive, and may actually stimulate him to
produce work of greater strength and concision. For Campion,
an accomplished artist in both media, the challenge of fitting
music and poetry to each other was probably beneficial, at least
to his poetry. Although the notion of music giving poetry an
extra dimension does not bear close inspection, it is clearly an
advantage for those who know a song and its words to be aware
of the separate impact that each has made. The harmony of
independent voices in contrapuntal music is one of the ways in
which the art can give most satisfaction. There is a similar occur-
rence, with similar potentialities, in the integration of words with
music. This is, of course, an essential feature of the art of Song.
When words and music are the work of one man we have the
additional interest of discovering his musical and verbal expression of the same mood, emotion or event. In *My sweetest
Lesbia, It fell on a sommers day* and *Vaine men whose follies make
a God of Love* (to name only three examples) the agreement of
words and music has a mastery that refreshes the hearer with
surprise and also with a sense of inevitability – the best symptoms,
perhaps, of artistic satisfaction. And the artistry is as much in the
fit of words to music as in words or music by themselves.

While the metrical shape of some of Campion's poems was
undoubtedly determined by the requirements of musical setting,
the music was influenced by the poetry in a more general way, in
particular by the selection of the homophonic lute song rather
than the polyphonic madrigal as his chief musical medium.
Nevertheless, he admitted and used polyphonic devices with
economy and decorum in some of his best songs (e.g. *It fell on a
sommers day* and *Author of light*). With the same discreet artistry
he adopted some of the ideas of the *Pléiade* without becoming a
slave to the rules of *musique mesurée*. Nor did he feel himself tied
to the rules of prosody which he explored and, apparently, purged
from his system in the *Observations in the Art of English Poesie*.

The other aspect of Campion's life which might be expected to have influenced his writing was the practice of medicine. This influence could appear in the form of imagery referring to disease and healing, or–at a deeper level–in the experience and understanding of human nature, and especially of human frailty. It would be hard to guess, from references of the former type, that Campion–or for that matter, Lodge, Vaughan, Goldsmith, Keats, Schiller, Beddoes and Bridges–practised or had, at least, studied, medicine. Perhaps Campion shows more influences of this kind than most other doctor-poets; in his fondness for imagery of wounds and healing, for example:

> Fountaine of health, my soules deepe wounds recure
>
> (I, 1)
>
> Their sinne-sicke soules by him shall be recured
>
> (I, 4)
>
> A wound long hid growes past recure
>
> (II, 6)

Pain and death are common subjects of poetry, but in Campion's writing they sometimes have a clinical air:

> Leave prolonging thy distresse:
> All delayes afflict the dying.
>
> (IV, 1)
>
> Thanks be to heav'n, no grievous smart,
> No maladies my limbes annoy.
>
> (IV, 21)

His spiritual view is hygienic, and he illustrates spiritual values by images of health and illness: e.g.

> But my soule still surfets so
> On the poysoned baytes of sinne,
> That I strange and ugly growe.
>
> (I, 5)
>
> Cold age deafes not there our eares, nor vapour dims our eyes.
>
> (I, 11)

Mental health and illness are the subject of other images; e.g.

> The first step to madnesse
> Is the excesse of sadnesse.
>
> (IV, 14)

Griefes past recure fooles try to heale.

(IV, 4)

'Tis their best med'cine that are pain'd
All thought to loose of past delight.

(IV, 16)

Such remarks are not specifically medical and might have been spoken by any educated person of the time. But it is, perhaps, significant that the twenty-one poems by Campion in Rosseter's *Booke of Ayres*, which were published several years before he took his medical degree, contain no references to wounds or healing, and very few images that suggest the impact of medical experience.

More important but less tangible influences of medical experience may, perhaps, be discovered in Campion's varied psychological observation. Half concealed under the amorous rhetoric of his time are many subtleties and gleams of insight. The course of true love is presented as a battle of wits and nerves. In sequences of poems the man and the woman each speak their minds and reveal a spectrum of moods ranging from depression to euphoria. They suffer the pangs of a divided mind (e.g. 'The same thing I seeke and flie', II, 14) and of uncertainty ('worse than paine is feare to mee', II, 6). The expression of moods and emotion is punctuated by aphoristic comments, sometimes seasoned with ironies and overtones that have a curiously modern tone: e.g.

Vaile, love, mine eyes; O hide from me
The plagues that charge the curious minde

(IV, 4)

Though Bryers breed Roses, none the Bryer affect.

(IV, 11)

So ev'ry day we live a day wee dye

(I, 17)

This is linked with an unsentimental and realistic view of human nature: e.g.

He that a true embrace will finde
To beauties faults must still be blinde.

(IV, 4)

Hee that courts us, wanting Arte, soon falters when he fayneth,
Lookes a-squint on his discourse, and smiles, when hee complaineth.

(IV, 18)

Men that but one Saint adore,
Make a shew of love to more

(III, 27)

Many passages like these show an understanding of human
behaviour and a habit of observing it with sympathy but objec-
tively, as though through a window. How much, if any, of this
understanding Campion owed to his medical experience can only
be guessed. There are fewer psychological subtleties in the poems
he published with Rosseter before he became a doctor; but the
poetry of a younger man might, in any case, be expected to
contain fewer things of this kind.

Perhaps the moments of dispassionate sagacity will eventually
be found to contribute little to our valuation of Campion. The
poems to which we return most often are, in fact, the simpler
and more directly lyrical ones that form the greater part of his
contribution to Rosseter's Book; these are also the poems most
appropriate for musical setting and, on the whole, most aptly set.
In spite of the wide span of Campion's attainments, he remained
a miniaturist, a master of limited range and intensity in each of
the forms that he attempted. His span is that of Shelley's Apollo
in claiming

All harmony of instruments or verse,
All prophecy, all medicine are mine;

but in spite of his integration of words and music and in spite of
the urbane philosophy of his later books, he was not

the eye with which the Universe
Beholds itself and knows itself divine.

His talents led him to a narrower world of brilliantly outlined
particulars in which sounds, both verbal and musical, share the
focus of interest with statements of epigrammatic lightness and
precision.

SELECT BIBLIOGRAPHY

EDITIONS OF CAMPION'S WORKS

Campion's Works, edited by Percival Vivian, Oxford, 1909.

The Works of Dr. Thomas Campion, edited by A. H. Bullen, London, Chiswick Press, 1889.

The Works of Thomas Campion, edited by Walter R. Davis, Doubleday and Co., New York, 1967, and Faber, 1969.

The Lyric Poems of Thomas Campion, edited by Ernest Rhys, Dent, 1895.

English Madrigal Verse, edited by E. H. Fellowes, 3rd edition, revised and enlarged by F. W. Sternfeld and D. Greer, Oxford, 1967.

Thomas Campion: Songs from Rosseter's Book of Airs (1601), Parts I and II, edited by E. H. Fellowes, in the English School of Lutenist Song Writers, Stainer & Bell, London, 1922.[1]

Thomas Campion: First Book of Airs (*circa* 1613), edited by E. H. Fellowes, Stainer & Bell, London, 1925.

Thomas Campion: Second Book of Airs (*circa* 1613), edited by E. H. Fellowes, Stainer & Bell, London, 1925.

Thomas Campion: Third Book of Airs (*circa* 1617), edited by E. H. Fellowes, Stainer & Bell, London, 1926.

Thomas Campion: Fourth Book of Airs (*circa* 1617), edited by E. H. Fellowes, Stainer & Bell, London, 1926.

A. J. Sabol (editor), *Songs and Dances for the Stuart Masque*, Providence, 1959.

BOOKS AND ARTICLES

R. W. Berringer, 'Thomas Campion's Share in A Booke of Ayres', in *PMLA*, Vol. 58, 1943, p. 938.

H. C. Colles, *Voice and Verse: A Study in English Song*, O.U.P., London, 1928.

J. P. Cutts, 'Jacobean Masque and Stage Music', in *Music & Letters*, London, Vol. 35, 1954, p. 185,

H. A. Evans (ed.), *English Masques*, Blackie, London, 1897.

Nigel Fortune, 'Solo Song and Cantata', in *The New Oxford History of Music*, Vol. IV, London, 1968, p. 125.

David Greer, ' "What if a day"–an Examination of the Words and the Music'; in *Music & Letters*, Vol. 43, 1962, p. 316.

[1] A new edition of this series is in preparation.

N

David Greer, 'Campion the Musician', in *The Lute Society Journal*, 1967, Vol. 9, p. 7.

David Greer, *The English Air*, Faber (in preparation).

Catherine Ing, *Elizabethan Lyrics*, Chatto & Windus, 1951.

R. W. Ingram, in *Elizabethan Poetry*, Stratford-upon-Avon Studies, 2, Edwin Arnold, London, 1960.

E. D. Jones (ed.), *English Critical Essays*, Oxford, 1943.

M. M. Kastendieck, *England's Musical Poet: Thomas Campion*, New York, O.U.P., 1938.

C. S. Lewis, *English Literature of the Sixteenth Century*, Oxford, 1954.

Edward Lowbury, 'Thomas Campion', in *The Concise Encyclopædia of English and American Poets and Poetry*, ed. S. Spender and D. Hall, Hutchinson, London, 1963.

Wilfrid Mellers, 'Words and Music in Elizabethan England', in *The Age of Shakespeare* (ed. B. Ford), Penguin Books, 1955.

Wilfrid Mellers, *Harmonious Meeting: a Study of Music, Poetry and Drama in England, 1600–1900*, Dobson, London, 1965.

Thomas Morley, *A Plain and Easy Introduction to Practical Music* (1597), edited by R. A. Harman, Dent, London, 1952.

Bruce Pattison, *Music and Poetry of the English Renaissance*, Methuen, London, 1948.

Gustave Reese, *Music in the Renaissance*, Dent, London, 1954.

R. W. Shortt, 'Campion's Metrics', in *PMLA*, 1944, Vol. 59, p. 1003.

C. J. Sisson (ed.), *Thomas Lodge and other Elizabethans*, Harvard University Press, 1933.

Hallett Smith, *Elizabethan Poetry*, Harvard University Press, 1952.

John Stevens, 'The Elizabethan Madrigal', in *Essays and Studies*, edited by B. Willey, Murray, London, 1958.

E. M. W. Tillyard, *The Elizabethan World Picture*, Chatto & Windus, 1952.

Peter Warlock, *The English Ayre*, O.U.P., London, 1926.

Enid Welsford, *The Court Masque: a study in the Relationship between Poetry and Revels*, Cambridge University Press, 1927.

L. P. Wilkinson, 'Propertius and Thomas Campion', in *London Magazine*, 1967, Vol. 7, p. 57.

INDEX

INDEX

NOTE. The titles of songs and poems are indicated by quotation marks, masques and books by italics.

Wolf, Hugo, 35, 46
'Wooe her and win her', 106, 108–9
Wooldridge, H. E., 11
Wordsworth, William, 10, 116, 148
Wyatt, Sir Thomas, 44

Yeats, W. B., 12, 144, 179
Yonge, Nicholas, 11
'Young and simple though I am',
    137, 151
'Your faire lookes', 71